# Helping Older Adults
# EXPERIENCING TRAUMATIC CRISIS

Dr. Dorothy L. Greenwood

Doctor in Ministry, Christian Counseling

# ACKNOWLEDGMENTS

"Bear ye another's burdens and so fulfill the Law of Christ" (Galatians 6:2).

My motto is, "If I can help somebody as I pass along, If I can cheer somebody with a word or song, If I can tell somebody they are going wrong then my living will not be in vain." Here, I must acknowledge and thank those who have done the same for me. I take this opportunity to give thanks and praise to my God for giving me the strength, courage, faith, ability, and the Spiritual Inspiration in writing this Biblical Manual. I want to applaud my instructors, Dr. Diana Morgan and Dr. Shirley Wood, for their tremendous efforts in guiding me in implementing and completing this Biblical Manual.

Special thanks are extended to my children and grand children who were always a tower of strength to me. They were very encouraging and gave me words of praise. For example, they would say, "Mommy you are not too old, go for it! The sky is the limit." Thank you, Alrick, Tracy, Fabia, Debrakaye Esquire: To God be the glory.

Special commendation to Bishop Dr. Kenneth Hill, Overseer for Southern New England Church of God churches and his wife, First Lady and ordained minister Janice Hill, for their input in my life their prayers and encouraging words were a tower of strength.

To my Bishop, Bishop Oral Roberts and his lovely wife Dr,. Olivia Roberts who were always persistent in encouraging, praying for and with me. Their credo was always "Woman of God: Go for it!" —a wish that was always accepted with sincerity. To all my friends, and church family you never leave me your words of prayers, encouragement was always welcomed. Special thanks to Lecia who would bring me my hot cooked bananas and salted fish and coconut run down, combing my hair, and seeking to find out in the nights if I am ok, also to Sis' Veronica

Sis' Pauline Beason and Joe Wills who would help me with quotes from the Bible and their words of encouragement.

Many thanks to Dr. Pacqua for introducing Dr. Norman Dale to me to edit the Manual. I appreciate your work, Dr. Dale, for even when my professor corrected, you were there to give instructions on how it should be done. Thanks again for the idea of the Messy Tool Kit. All God's blessings upon your life, Dr. Dale.

To Dr. Melissa-Sue John of Lauren Simone Publishing House, I extend special thanks for your efforts in publishing this Biblical Manual, I pray for God's blessings and prosperity in your daily endeavors.

Again, I thank God, IT'S finished!! IT'S completed!!! IT'S DONE!!!!!!

# Table of Contents

LIST OF TABLES.................................................................................................................III

LIST OF FIGURES ..............................................................................................................V

SYNOPSIS ........................................................................................................................1

PART 1: INTRODUCTION ...................................................................................................3

    Understanding Geriatrics and the Aging Process .............................................................4

    Steps in Providing Effective Counseling..........................................................................5

    PTSD and the Aging Population......................................................................................6

    Traumatic Experiences in Older Populations ..................................................................8

    Overview of Christian Counseling ..................................................................................8

    Understanding Biblical Counseling ...............................................................................10

PART II. THE COUNSELING PROCESS...............................................................................12

    Initial Session ..............................................................................................................13

    Process of Change ........................................................................................................16

PART III. TECHNIQUES FOR WORKING WITH OLDER ADULTS

EXPERIENCING TRAUMATIC CRISIS ................................................................................19

    Prayer..........................................................................................................................19

    Bible Study ..................................................................................................................19

    Reflection ....................................................................................................................21

    Encouragement ............................................................................................................22

    Confession ...................................................................................................................22

    Listening .....................................................................................................................24

PART IV. BIBLICAL AND OTHER TECHNIQUES FOR CHRISTIAN COUNSELORS.........26

    Teachings of Jesus and the Bible..................................................................................26

    Case Study...................................................................................................................26

    Approaches to Christian Counseling for Older Adults: Use of Non-Religious Therapies.....28

    Conclusion...................................................................................................................36

PART V. SPIRITUAL CARE FOR OLDER ADULTS EXPERIENCING      TRAUMATIC

CRISIS ...........................................................................................................................38

Establishing a Safe, Respectful, and Supportive Environment ...................................................38

Link Between Spirituality and Religion .................................................................................39

Spiritual and Religious Coping .............................................................................................41

Effects of Spirituality-Religion on Health..............................................................................43

Spiritual Distress and Defensive Behaviors ..........................................................................45

Outreach Care Programs and Other Activities ......................................................................50

PART VI.BRIEF CASES ...............................................................................................................56

Case 1—Eleanor: Lack of a Sense of Purpose/Motivation ...................................................56

Case 2—John: Coping With a Traumatic Event.....................................................................57

Case 3—Mary: Struggling with Depression and Anxiety After Loss ....................................58

Case 4—Joseph: Facing Loneliness and Depression .............................................................59

Case 5—Sara: Dealing with Chronic Pain ............................................................................60

Case 6—James: Facing the Loss of Faith...............................................................................60

PART VII: A TOOLKIT FOR PASTORAL COUNSELING .....................................................62

1. Substantive Challenges Faced by the Client.....................................................................64

2. Theoretical Bases of Counselling .....................................................................................79

3. Specific Techniques of Intervention .................................................................................93

4. Biblically-Based Counselling Techniques ......................................................................107

5. Specific Skills for Counselling Practice .........................................................................110

CONCLUSION ............................................................................................................................127

WORKS CITED AND CONSULTED .........................................................................................128

# List of Tables

Table 1. Sequence of Steps in the Counseling Process ................................................. 12

Table 2. Primary Factors that Shape Religious and Spiritual Practices ....................................... 40

Table 3. Some Aspects of Positive and Negative Coping of Spiritualityand Religion ................. 43

Table 4. Index for The Toolkit for Pastoral Counseling................................................ 62

# List of Figures

Figure 1. The Three Phases of Salvation ........................................................................... 10

Figure 2. Pott's Diagram of the Change Process in Counseling ..................................... 17

Figure 3. Balancing the Elements of Attention to the Unique Needs of Patients to Empower Resources On Spiritual/Religious Coping ....................................................... 36

Figure 4. The Messy Reality of Biblical Counseling Elements of Practice ....

Figure 5. A Couple Looking At The Ruins Of Their House Destroyed By Fire ........... 71

Figure 6. Turning the Hermeneutical Circle into a Spiral ............................................ 81

Figure 7. Diagram of Therapist/Client Process ........................................................... 83

Figure 8. Range of Aims for Pastoral Care ............................                                    .

Figure 9. Elements of Applying Adlerian Therapy to Counseling and Healing ........... 87

Figure 10. Key Elements of Mindfulness Practice ....................................................... 92

Figure 11. Actions in Relation to the Experience of Loneliness and Stress ....

Figure 12. Element of Solution-Focused Brief Therapy ............................................... 88

Figure 13. A Model of Counseling for Grief and Loss ................................................. 66

Figure 14. Prayer During Counseling Session With Dr. Rickey Nation ..................... 115

1

# SYNOPSIS

Any traumatic event, whether it be a natural disaster on a global scale or a personal tragedy, can have a profound effect on a person. The fact that many people in our modern society are experiencing spiritual crises is not news. Nonetheless, one should not give up hope. Learn how to soothe a battered spirit and restore its equilibrium with the help of Spiritual Crisis: Overcoming Trauma to the Soul. When you take a holistic, practical approach to spiritual care, you gain the insight you need to put a stop on the daily chaos that threatens to ruin people whose lives have been broken by tragedy, fear, and disappointment. This handbook is designed to serve as a practical guide for Christian counselors and pastors who care for older adults experiencing traumatic crises. It provides an overview of Christian counseling, outlines the counseling process, offers techniques for working with older adults, and includes brief case studies and vignettes for training and guidance in practice.

The handbook also explores spiritual care for older adults, including the role of faith, prayer, and contemplative practices. The manual begins with an introduction to the purpose and overview of Christian counseling. It then moves on to a discussion of the counseling process, providing information about the initial session, assessing the client, and setting goals. It also covers a range of techniques for working with older adults, including mind-body therapy, cognitive behavioral therapy, dialectical behavior therapy, and the emotional freedom technique.

Additionally, the handbook covers spiritual care for older adults, such as the role of faith, prayer, and contemplative practices. The largest section of the handbook is a discussion of a wide array of topics that comprise what I have called a "Toolkit for Pastoral Counsellors." This is organized into five sections although there is substantial overlap in the "tools." This manual allows Christian counselors and pastors to provide effective and compassionate care to those experiencing a traumatic crisis. As Frederick Buechner wrote, "The place God calls you to is the place where your deep gladness and the world's deep hunger meet.'"" (22). This handbook seeks to equip and empower counselors and pastors to meet the spiritual and emotional needs of older adults in crisis. The manual presents case studies to illustrate the application of these techniques followed by a conclusion summarizing the key points, exploring future directions, and providing valuable resources.

## PART 1: INTRODUCTION

Christian therapy is a therapeutic approach that takes a Christian worldview and applies it to all aspects of a client's life including their mind, body, and spirit. Therefore, it is a vital component of good health and a powerful resource for assisting those through a stressful situation. This handbook is dedicated to assisting Christian counselors in working with older adults struggling with traumatic concerns. It provides an overview of the counseling process, describes different techniques for working with older adults, and gives an overview of spiritual care for those dealing with a traumatic crisis. Case studies are also included to help practitioners apply the concepts to their practice.

The scripture states, "The Lord is near to the brokenhearted and saves the crushed in spirit" (Psalm 34:18). This handbook will show that, with the right tools, we can provide hope, healing, and comfort to those who are in need. The Bible's statement in Psalm 34:18 is a powerful reminder that those who are brokenhearted and crushed in spirit can find comfort and hope through Christian counseling. This manual seeks to equip Christian counselors with the knowledge and skills needed to provide comfort and respect to those dealing with traumatic crises. As theologian Paul Tillich once said, "The courage to be is the courage to accept oneself, despite being unacceptable" (Garabedian 2). Through techniques such as mind-body therapy, cognitive behavioral therapy, dialectical behavior therapy, emotional freedom technique, and spiritual care such as prayer and contemplative practices, Christian counselors can work with older adults to help them move through their traumatic crisis.

Additionally, case studies are included in this manual to help counselors understand how to apply the concepts to their own practice. This manual is based on the work of Eleanor O'Leary in *Counseling Troubled Older Adults*, Everett Worthington in *A Christian Approach to Counseling*, James Ellor in *Aging and Spirituality*, and Gary Kennedy in *Mental Health Care*. Data from the

Substance Abuse and Mental Health Department of the Health and the National Centre on Elder Abuse have also been incorporated.

Ultimately, this manual is meant to help Christian counselors provide the healing, hope, and comfort of those in need seek. Using it, counselors can help those struggling with traumatic crises find relief, strength, and peace. I will provide an overview of the counseling process, describe various techniques for working with older adults, and give an overview of spiritual care for those dealing with a traumatic crisis. By understanding the unique needs of older adults coping with traumatic problems, Christian counselors can provide the healing, hope, and comfort that those in need seek. .

**Understanding Geriatrics and the Aging Process**

Then the Lord God said, "See! The man has become like one of us, knowing what is good and what is bad! This is why we can't let him reach out and take an apple from the tree of eternal life, lest he eat it and live forever." Therefore, the Lord God cast him out of the Garden of Eden and made him work the soil of his original home. Having banished man from Eden, God placed him to the east of the garden and posted the cherubim and the flaming rotating sword there to protect the entrance to the tree of life—Genesis 3:22–24.

The aging process can be a difficult one for many seniors, with feelings of loss and uncertainty often accompanying the transition from young adulthood to old age. These feelings can be compounded when a senior is faced with a traumatic crisis, such as an illness or the death of a loved one. It is at times like these that Christian counseling—as provided in this manual—can be a valuable resource for seniors, providing guidance and support that can help them cope with their difficult situation.

Although some mature adults may look forward to their "Golden Years" because of things like retirement, grandkids, or just a new stage of life, others may fear the cognitive and physical decline that comes with getting older. Many older people may find it challenging to adjust to retirement, manage newfound frailty or medical concerns, or discover pleasurable, meaningful hobbies if they are limited in their mobility. Some elderly people may have a hard time accepting death, especially after the loss of close friends, peers, spouses, and partners, which can lead to feelings of solitude.

Older adults are those over the age of 65. As they grow older, they may experience physical, mental, and emotional changes that can be difficult to adjust to. Additionally, they may face the loss of loved ones, financial and emotional worries, and other crises that can be overwhelming. Older adults have unique needs that must be considered in Christian counseling. These include physical, emotional, and spiritual needs.

Older adults may be more vulnerable to physical illnesses and may need more intensive medical care. In addition, they may be more susceptible to physical pain and fatigue, making it important for the counselor to be aware of their needs and be prepared to adjust the counseling session accordingly.

The emotional needs of older adults are often very different from those of younger adults, ranging from feelings of loneliness or sadness to anxiety or depression. Older adults often have a strong spiritual connection and may look to their faith for comfort and guidance during difficult times. The counselor should be sensitive to these emotions and be prepared to help the elderly individual find ways to manage them.

**Steps in Providing Effective Counseling**

Effective counseling can be seen as involving four key steps: establishing a rapport, identifying the problem, developing an action plan, and supporting the individual.

*Step 1: Establishing Rapport*

Establishing a strong rapport with the older adult is essential for providing effective counseling. The counselor should be patient, empathetic, and respectful of the individual's unique needs and experiences. This can be done by asking questions, listening to their stories, and helping them find solutions to their problems.

*Step 2: Identifying the Problem*

It is important for the counselor to identify the cause of the traumatic crisis the older adult is experiencing. The counselor should ask questions to gain a better understanding of the problem and explore potential solutions.

*Step 3: Developing an Action Plan*

Once the problem has been identified, the counselor should work with the older adult to develop an action plan. This plan should include steps to address the individual's physical, emotional, and spiritual needs. It should also include a timeline and resources available to the individual.

*Step 4: Supporting the Individual*

The counselor should provide ongoing support for the older adult throughout the process. This can include providing encouragement, offering reassurance, and helping the individual stay on track with their action plan.

**PTSD and the Aging Population**

The mental health of the elderly is routinely disregarded. This is a problem since people of retirement age experience mental health problems at the same rate as people of any other age group. In terms of mental illness, PTSD is extremely prevalent among the elderly (PTSD). Someone can develop PTSD after being exposed to a stressful incident, such as a natural disaster, an automobile accident, or an act of violence. Long-term stressful situations, including taking care of a loved one who has a chronic condition, might also set it off. The effects of post-traumatic stress disorder on the wellbeing of the elderly are significant. Stress, melancholy, and social withdrawal are all possible outcomes. It can also impede attempts to control long-term medical issues. For older folks, PTSD treatment is crucial. The elderly are notoriously reluctant to seek care for mental health difficulties, which is a major public health crisis. Insufficient knowledge about mental illness and its treatment is often to blame (Martin et al.).

Seniors suffering from post-traumatic stress disorder may benefit from engaging in Christian counseling. Seniors who seek the help of a Christian counselor may find comfort and direction in their time of need. They can also aid senior citizens in establishing beneficial coping practices. When it comes to healing from trauma, Christian counseling can provide a warm and accepting environment for seniors. While PTSD can occur at any age, there are some unique challenges that come with treating older adults with this disorder. One of the most important things to keep in mind when treating older adults with PTSD is that they are more likely to have comorbid medical conditions. This means that they may be taking multiple medications that could interact with each other or with any new medications prescribed for the treatment of PTSD. In addition, older adults may have cognitive impairments that make it difficult for them to process and understand information about their trauma. It is also important to consider the social context in which older adults live. As discussed by McGwin et al., many older adults are retired and may live alone, which can increase feelings of isolation and loneliness.

While there are challenges associated with treating older adults with PTSD, there are also many benefits to using a Christian or biblical counseling approach. Christian counseling focuses on the whole person, including their spiritual needs. This can be especially helpful for older adults, who may be struggling with issues of meaning and purpose in their lives. In addition, Christian counseling emphasizes the importance of relationships, which can be beneficial for older adults who are often isolated. Finally, Christian counseling approaches typically emphasize hope and healing, which can be very helpful for individuals who are struggling with the effects of trauma.

**Traumatic Experiences in Older Populations**

The history of biblical counseling and trauma in older adults has been one where counselors have increasingly focused on the unique needs of this population. In recent years, there has been a greater focus on understanding and addressing the needs of older adults who have experienced trauma. This has led to a better understanding of how-to best support and care for this population.

Older adults have often experienced a lifetime of trauma, including violence, war, natural disasters, and childhood abuse. These experiences can have a major impact on their mental and physical health. Counselors who work with older adults need to be aware of the potential for trauma and its effects. They also need to be prepared to help older adults heal from their trauma and to support them in their recovery.

**Overview of Christian Counseling**

Religious counseling is a therapeutic approach that takes a Christian worldview and applies it to all aspects of a client's life, including their mind, body, and spirit. It aims to meet the needs of the full person, not just the symptoms of illness. Accordingly, Christian counseling is an important aspect of a healthy lifestyle and a useful resource for those going through difficult times.[1]

Different methods and approaches are used in Christian counseling, including cognitive behavior therapy (CBT), dialectical behavior therapy (DBT), and emotionally focused therapy (EFT). Christian therapy places a premium on spiritual care, which might include prayer and other contemplative practices. Christian counseling also creates a safe and supportive environment for those seeking help including making a safe space where clients can feel comfortable sharing their

---

[1] This point is elaborated on by Worthington in his book about Christian counseling for couples.

thoughts and feelings and find acceptance and understanding. Additionally, as O'Leary describes, Christian counselors strive to provide a non-judgmental and compassionate atmosphere in which clients can explore their feelings and make changes in their lives.

Christian counseling is a form of counseling that has been used for centuries to help individuals dealing with traumatic crises. Scholars such as Eleanor O'Leary, Everett Worthington, and Gary Kennedy have conducted extensive research in this area. They have identified the key elements of Christian counseling necessary for helping individuals who are dealing with a traumatic crisis. For example, O'Leary states that counselors must be "attentive, compassionate, and respectful" (23) when working with older adults experiencing traumatic crises Similarly, Worthington emphasizes the importance of helping individuals understand the power of faith and prayer to help them overcome their traumatic crisis (Worthington 45). Finally, Kennedy (156) notes that counselors must assess older adults' mental health and provide treatment when necessary.

In addition to the work of O'Leary, Worthington, and Kennedy, there are several other resources that can be helpful for Christian counselors working with older adults experiencing a traumatic crisis. The American Association of Christian Counselors (AACC) is an excellent resource for counselors and provides information on best practices for working with older adults. Additionally, the National Institute on Aging (NIA) provides information and resources for those seeking to learn more about caring for older adults experiencing traumatic crises. The Substance Abuse & Mental Health Treatments Administration (SAMHSA) offers data and materials concerning mental health services for the elderly.

Ultimately, Christian counseling is a powerful tool for helping those in need. It offers a compassionate and supportive environment, as well as techniques and approaches that can be used to help those dealing with traumatic crises. This handbook is designed to equip Christian counselors with the knowledge and skills needed to provide this kind of help to older adults.

**Understanding Biblical Counseling**

Christian counseling is a form of therapy that focuses on an individual's spiritual journey. For older adults who are experiencing a traumatic crisis, this type of counseling can be especially beneficial. This manual will explain the three phases of salvation, discuss techniques for helping older adults, and provide resources for further learning.

*The Three Phases of Salvation*

Salvation can best be understood in terms of three phases—past, present, and future (See Figure 1).

Fig. 1. The Three
Phases of Salvation

The past phase of salvation focuses on acknowledging God's grace and forgiveness in the past. This involves recognizing the power of God's mercy and grace in our lives and reflecting on how our past experiences have shaped us. It also involves letting go of guilt and shame and accepting that we can be forgiven and redeemed.

The present phase of salvation emphasizes living in the present moment and recognizing God's presence in the here and now. This involves developing a deeper and more meaningful relationship with Christ by praying, studying the Bible, and practicing spiritual disciplines such as fasting and meditation. It also consists in recognizing God's grace and love in our current circumstances and trusting in his plan for our lives.

The future phase of salvation focuses on looking forward to the life that awaits us after we pass on, trusting in God's guidance and love to bring us to our ultimate destination. This involves looking forward to life in heaven and trusting God's promises and the ultimate plan. It also involves understanding our purpose in life and living in a way that honors God and brings glory to his name.

Christian counseling can be an invaluable tool when helping older adults in crisis. By understanding the three phases of salvation and using techniques such as listening, providing emotional support, and discussing Scripture and faith, counselors can help their clients find hope and peace in difficult times. Finally, the resources provided in this manual can be used to explore this topic further and learn more about Christian counseling for older adults in crisis.

## PART II. THE COUNSELING PROCESS

The sequence of parts of the counseling process is summarized in Table 1. In the following discussion I rely significantly on Weidmann's outline of steps in the process.

**Table 1**

*Sequence of Steps in the Counseling Process*

| Biblical Counseling Process |
|---|
| STEP 1: INVOLVEMENT |
| *Goal:* To create an environment where you feel safe sharing your struggles and failures. |
| A Biblical Counselor does not simply want to solve your problem but become your friend. As a friend, your counselor will express genuine concern for you and your issues. As a part of the biblical counseling process, each session will include time for talking and praying together. |
| STEP 2: INVESTIGATION |
| *Goal:* To have an accurate understanding of the problem. |
| According to Proverbs 18:13, it's a sign of foolishness and disgrace to reply before listening. It's important to remember that your counselor can't help you until he hears you out first.<br>More time will be spent on the inquiry during the first few sessions of biblical counseling. For your biblical counselor to get to the bottom of your problems, he or she will ask a lot of questions.<br>Being truthful and open is essential at this stage. Your counselor won't be able to help you as much as he could if he must guess at the source of your problems. Do not let inhibitions or self-consciousness keep you from sharing your challenges with others. |
| STEP 3: INSTRUCTION |
| *Goal:* To apply the biblical solution to your problem. |
| Giving biblical instruction is the next step in biblical counseling. The teaching will not only be relevant to your current situation but will also be tailored to address the concerns in your heart.<br>Since the Bible will be our primary source of information, please bring it with you each week. In order to grow into a person who puts God's Word into practice in their own lives, you will study biblical examples, memorize Scripture, and complete homework tasks. |
| STEP 4: IMPLEMENTATION |
| *Goal:* The counselor will hold you accountable to grow and change by implementing what you have learned during the counseling session. |
| The fourth step in biblical counseling is putting the plan into action. To be "doers" of the Word, and not just "hearers," is what we are commanded to do throughout the Bible. Your biblical counselor will give you assignments to help you put into practice the principles you discuss in sessions. |

| Biblical Counseling Process |
| :--- |
| Between sessions, you will do much of the heavy lifting that goes into counseling. Topical research, Scripture memorizing, habit modification, letter writing, computer filter setup, etc., are all fair game for homework assignments. |

## Initial Session

The initial session of biblical counseling can actually be the hardest one for both the counsellor and the counselee. Weidmann in an insightful discussion of this first encounter comments "A first session in biblical counseling can be intimidating. Even the best Certified Biblical Counselors can experience some nervousness when meeting with a person for the first time." This is not surprising since what is about to happen is intimate disclosure and exploration of matters close to very essence of the older person's life. Fear and modesty are appropriate reactions on both sides, but Weidmann reassures, "we can proceed with confidence in Christ and use God's Word to guide us. If the counselor is wise, slow to speak, and does not give an answer before she or he hears, we can have a vibrant counseling ministry" (para. 1). Some of the essentials that I want to cover in the opening session now follow.

### *Opening the Session*

As the session begins, high on the "agenda" of every counselee is going to be finding out more about that person who is sitting with them and to whom one's deepest thoughts and fears are soon to be shared. Weidmann advises, "I strive to (1) explain who I am and how I plan to serve the counselee; (2) explain what biblical counseling means and the hopeful outcome for them; and (3) the expectation of them in the process. Weidmann goes on to raise a note of caution based on a well-known case that became a subject of litigation: "By setting the expectations of the biblical counseling they will experience it can avoid legal pitfalls" (that could cause the counselee to act upon misinterpretations of the relationship and what it offers. In a case eventually decided by the Supreme Court, the family of a man who eventually committed suicide tried to hold clergy responsible, a conflict rooted in the lack of clarity over what biblically based counseling can and cannot be responsible for.[1] Weidmann continued that he needs to be "honest with my counselee about what I am and am not going to do as a counselor (Ephesians. 4:25). I will promise them that I will listen to them. I will also promise to do my best to communicate what God's Word says about whatever they tell me. If I fail to do either, I invite them to ask me, correct me, or gain clarity."

### Build a Relationship

After the preliminaries of getting to know each other must come an even more challenging period dedicated to building a strong and trusting relationship. This is not a simple matter, given the imbalance in authority between a certified biblical counsellor and a person who, by definition, is going through difficult times. Patience is essential as Proverbs 18:13 insists: "To answer before listening—that is folly and shame" (NIV). Weidmann suggests that other Bible verses have much to teach counselors as they build the relationship: "I will ask them to be . . . teachable (Proverbs. 1-9), timely, and complete their homework between sessions. I want them to see their involvement as essential for their growth. By building a loving relationship in their life (Proverbs. 27.9), I can develop a meaningful relationship with them to minister God's Word (1 Thessalonians 2:7-9). Other than the obvious aim of bringing hope through insight is to acquaint the counselee with the very idea of relying on scriptures for confronting everyday challenges. When they reach that understanding, the Bible becomes a major resource for living and healing.

### Gather Relevant Data

The first session plays an essential role in providing a counselor with relevant data from the counselee's life. It is especially important to learn how religion has figured in their life story to this point. Weidmann says, "I will work hard to ask appropriate questions and carefully listen to the

---

[1] Savage provides an overview of this legal case and the aftermath of the Supreme Court decision.

counselee to understand what has occurred in their life. I will ask them to share their testimony about their faith in Jesus Christ." Usually, even this first session begins to reveal critical moments as well as chronic patterns that the counselee has come to employ as they face life's difficulties: the counselor must become fully aware of these if they are to help and advise. Weidmann adds, "I will strive to determine their receptivity to the Word of God. . . . I am keenly aware that I cannot give good counsel if I do not assess the facts of the counselee's situation. I must gain understanding before imparting wisdom" (Prov. 18:13, 17).

### *Evaluate the Presenting Problem Biblically*

People coming to counseling are looking for hope. If I can identify their problem(s) biblically and impart wisdom through a relationship centered on respect and love, there is a better chance that counselees will devise and implement good changes to alleviate their problems. Weidmann suggests, that "by separating the problem(s) into proper categories, I will have the opportunity to show the robustness of God's Word and explain how God speaks to each aspect of their life (James. 4:1-4). This is how I can establish goals for future sessions.

### *Provide Biblical Instruction and Insight*

I aim counseling to equip the counselee with practical insights about the word of God (Rom. 12:1-2) and give them wisdom about living so that the Lord is pleased. I must build on what I learned from data-gathering to present them with solutions consistent with biblical teachings. My help and guidance must be based on the Bible for my work to be authentic biblical counseling. these sessions it is also important to *pray together*: Praying together as a counselor and client sets the tone for the session and invites the power of God into the room. This establishes the fact that it is the Lord who heals and restores.

*Assign Relevant Homework*

Each counseling session should close with homework that advances the counselee's ability to apply what we covered. This supports the counselee bring the Word of God to their daily life. Only this will bring "moments of life [to] be lived out with God for lasting change" (Weidmann). The session by itself cannot bring about change—the "homework" of living and acting differently is essential. As Weidmann concluded, "God must be a part of their daily life; the work done between sessions will drive towards this end of a closer and continual walk with Jesus Christ" (James-1:22-23).

*Schedule the Next Session*

If the session has proven to be rewarding from the counselee's perspective, it is important to schedule the next session. Doing so not only is important logistically but reinforces the mutual obligations to carry on into the future with the counseling process. Assuming that this session was fruitful, and all elements of counseling standards were maintained, I will ask the counselee to schedule another session. It is a necessary part of the bonding and leaves both counselor and counselee in hopeful and confident that the new relationship will be fruitful and continuing. Closing with a prayer for God to bring healing and restoration to the person's life [is] my usual way of finalizing the first session.

## Process of Change

Pastor Jeff Potts, in his work at Canyon Hills Counseling, has conceptualized the change process as shown in Figure 2.

# PROCESS OF CHANGE

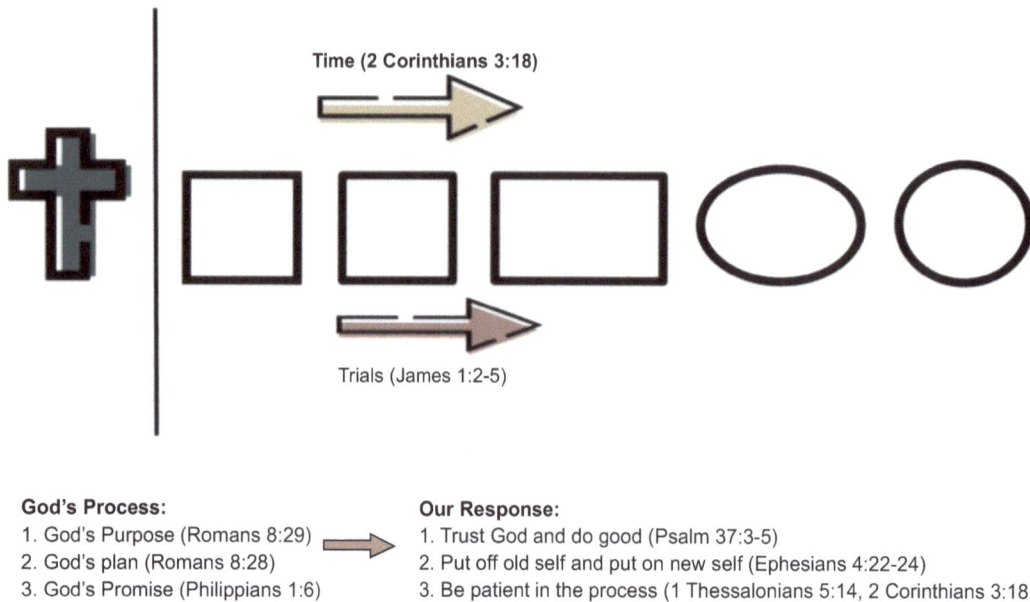

Time (2 Corinthians 3:18)

Trials (James 1:2-5)

**God's Process:**
1. God's Purpose (Romans 8:29)
2. God's plan (Romans 8:28)
3. God's Promise (Philippians 1:6)

**Our Response:**
1. Trust God and do good (Psalm 37:3-5)
2. Put off old self and put on new self (Ephesians 4:22-24)
3. Be patient in the process (1 Thessalonians 5:14, 2 Corinthians 3:18)

Fig. 2. Pott's Diagram of the Change Process in Counseling. Canyon Hills, "Biblical Counseling Diagrams." https://www.canyonhillscounseling.org/diagrams-1

Change during counseling can be further described in terms of seven stages:

*Stage 1—Unawareness:* In this stage, the individual is unaware of the problem and the need for change. This is a crucial stage for counselors to assess the individual's understanding of the issue and identify any misinformation or resistance to change.

*Stage 2—Precontemplation*: In this stage, the individual has begun to identify the issue and the need for change but has yet to be willing to take action. Counselors can help the individual to see the need for change, explore their feelings and beliefs around the issue, and help them to explore potential strategies for change.

*Stage 3—Contemplation*: In this stage, the individual is considering making a change but is still uncertain. Counselors can help the individual explore the pros and cons of making a change, develop an action plan, and identify potential barriers to change.

*Stage 4—Separation*: In this stage, the individual has begun to take action and is actively preparing for the change. Counselors can help the individual to develop an action plan, identify resources, and develop self-care strategies to support them through the change process.

*Stage 5—Action*: In this stage, the individual actively takes steps to make the change. Counselors can provide support, feedback, and guidance to help the individual stay on track and make the necessary changes.

*Stage 6—Maintenance*: In this stage, the individual is maintaining the change and actively working to make it permanent. Counselors can help the individual identify potential relapse triggers and develop strategies to prevent relapse.

*Stage 7—Relapse*: In this stage, the individual has lost momentum and is at risk of returning to the previous behavior. Counselors can help the individual to identify the factors that led to the relapse and develop strategies for getting back on track.

By understanding each stage of change, counselors can provide appropriate support to individuals experiencing traumatic crises as they make meaningful changes.

## PART III. TECHNIQUES FOR WORKING WITH OLDER ADULTS EXPERIENCING TRAUMATIC CRISIS

The Bible provides a wealth of information and guidance to help people of all ages, including older adults, who are struggling with a traumatic crisis. Several biblical techniques are particularly beneficial for Christian counseling for older adults: prayer; Bible study (and the application of biblical lessons to practical life situations), reflection, encouragement, and confession.

**Prayer**

Praying for the older adult is one of the most important ways to provide spiritual guidance and support. Praying for healing, comfort, and strength can help the older adult regain peace and hope.

*Case Study on Prayer*. John, an elderly gentleman in his eighties, had just lost his wife of 60 years. He was struggling with deep grief and despair. During a counseling session, John was encouraged to pray for strength and comfort. He was asked to take moments throughout the day to pray for healing and peace. He was also encouraged to remember the good times he had shared with his wife and to give thanks for their time together. After a few weeks of prayer, John began feeling peace and joy in his heart. His faith and trust in God were restored.

"Come to me, all you who are weary and burdened, and I will give you rest. Take my yoke upon you and learn from me, for I am gentle and humble in heart, and you will find rest for your souls. For my yoke is easy and my burden is light." (Matthew 11:28-30).

**Bible Study**

Studying the Bible together can give older adults spiritual guidance and insight into how God can help them through their traumatic crisis. The Bible is a source of comfort and guidance for many people, especially older adults facing a traumatic situation. Christian counseling for older adults can use various biblical techniques to help them cope and find peace.

One technique is to draw on the teachings of Jesus to provide comfort and understanding. Jesus's parables are a great source of comfort, as He often used them to provide examples of how to live a better life. Jesus also gave great insights into how to handle suffering and grief. For example, in the parable of the Good Samaritan, Jesus taught that we should have compassion and love for our neighbors. This is an excellent reminder for older adults in crisis that they are not alone and that there is still hope for them.

Another biblical technique is to use the Psalms to provide comfort and solace. The Psalms are filled with beautiful verses that can be used to encourage and inspire older adults in their time of need. For example, Psalm 23:4 says, "Even though I walk through the darkest valley, I will fear no evil, for You are with me; Your rod and Your staff, they comfort me." This verse can comfort an older adult in a traumatic crisis, as it reminds them that even in the darkest times, God is still with them.

Finally, Christian counseling for older adults can draw on the teachings of Paul to provide guidance and understanding. Paul's letters provide a great source of wisdom and insight into how to face difficult situations. For example, in his letter to the Philippians, Paul teaches us to "Rejoice in the Lord always; again, I will say, rejoice" (Philippians 4:4). This verse provides an important reminder that even amid a crisis, we can still find joy and peace in the Lord.

*Case Study 1 on Bible Study*. The case studies in the book, Koening Counseling Older Adults, offer examples of how these biblical techniques can be applied in real-life situations. In one case, an older woman was struggling with the death of her husband. The counselor drew on Jesus's parables to provide comfort and understanding. He reminded her of the parable of the prodigal son, which teaches us that no matter how far we have strayed, God's love is always available to us. The counselor also used the Psalms to provide comfort and hope to the woman and Paul's letters to provide guidance and direction.

*Case Study 2 on Bible Study.* In another case, an older man was struggling with the death of his wife. The counselor drew on Jesus's parables to provide comfort and understanding. He reminded the man of the parable of the Good Samaritan, which teaches us that we should have compassion and love for our neighbors. The counselor also used the Psalms to provide comfort and solace to the man and Paul's letters to provide guidance and direction.

These case studies demonstrate how Christian counseling for older adults can draw on the Bible to provide comfort, solace, and guidance in times of crisis. By using these biblical techniques, counselors can help older adults to find peace and hope in their time of need.

**Reflection**

Reflection is essential for spiritual growth and helps older adults process and make sense of their emotions and experiences.

*Case Study on Reflection.* Ed is an older man who experienced a traumatic event. He is struggling to make sense of it and is feeling overwhelmed by all the emotions he is experiencing. The Christian counselor begins by encouraging Ed to reflect on the event. She helps him to identify the emotions that he is feeling and to think through the event from a spiritual perspective. The counselor then helps Ed to understand how his faith can help him process the trauma. She helps him to see how the Bible can be a foundation of comfort and guidance. She encourages Ed to reflect on his experiences and how they fit into his faith. The counselor also helps Ed to understand that his emotions are normal and valid. She helps him to identify healthy coping strategies and to develop a plan for managing his emotions. Finally, she enables him to recognize the strength that his faith can provide in times of difficulty. By helping Ed to reflect on his traumatic experience from a spiritual perspective, the Christian counselor has provided him with valuable insight and guidance. This has enabled Ed to gain a greater understanding of his emotions and to develop healthy coping strategies.

**Encouragement**

Giving older adults encouragement, hope, and love can help them find peace and healing.

*Case Study on Encouragement*. John is an 80-year-old man who is facing a traumatic crisis. His wife recently passed away, and he is struggling to cope. He is feeling lonely and overwhelmed. His pastor has referred him to a Christian counselor. The counselor begins by listening to John's story and validating his feelings. The counselor then encourages John to find strength in his faith and to look to God for comfort. The counselor reminds John that God loves and is with him, even in his darkest times. The counselor also encourages John to take small daily steps to help him heal, such as taking a walk or attending a support group.

John is grateful for the counselor's encouragement and begins to find peace and healing in his faith. The counselor continues to meet with John over the next few months, providing a listening ear and words of encouragement. John eventually begins to feel better and finds comfort in knowing God is with him through his grief.

**Confession**

Confessing and repenting of wrongdoings can help the older adult find forgiveness and peace.

*Case Study on Confession*. Joe is a war veteran who is struggling with being able to cope with his traumatic experiences. He is often overwhelmed with guilt and shame and struggles to find peace. Joe begins meeting with a Christian counselor and starts working through his past with the help of biblical counseling. Joe can confess his wrongdoings through counseling sessions and ask for forgiveness. The counselor can also help guide Joe through the process of repentance, which allows him to begin to find peace. In addition to confessing and repenting of wrongdoings, it is also essential to discuss the war veteran's traumatic experiences. The counselor can help the older adult process the trauma and provide emotional support. The counselor can also help the older adult learn healthy coping mechanisms and provide resources to help with managing their trauma. It is also essential to recognize that it is not possible to "undo" the traumatic experiences, but it is possible to learn how to cope and find healing. Joe can eventually move forward and find hope in his journey to recovery.

As the counselee does this, four practical efforts should be encouraged: forgiveness, comfort, guidance and listening.

*Forgiveness:* Forgiving those who have hurt older adults can help them find freedom to move forward. The Lord's Prayer, as related in Luke 11:4 says, "And forgive us of our sin; for we also forgive every one that is indebted to us" (KJV). The key is we must forgive others in order to be forgiven. Counselors should encourage the older adult to forgive and not hold on to a grudge or hatred in their hearts against anyone who does them harm. Forgiveness can bring peace and comfort to the soul.

*Comfort:* Providing comfort and support to the older adults can help them feel safe and secure. Psalm 95 speaks to the fact that in times of trouble God will hide you in His Pavillion in His secret place He will hide you. Nothing can harm you; no evil can come near you because you are sheltered, covered, protected by God. The song says you'll find rest in the eye of the storm. Older adults need to know that when they are in traumatic crisis there is someone in their lives to encourage them to comfort them to show them the right way.

**Guidance**

Guiding older Adults can help them make sense of their experiences and develop a plan for their future. Exodus 23:20 declares that the Lord will bring one's life to a new season of favor: "Behold I send an angel to keep thee in the way and to bring thee into the place I have prepared" (KJV). This plan of favor for the older Adults can only be developed or achieved by guidance of

God through his word and the Holy Spirit. 2 Corinthians 1:4 says that God "comforteth us in all our tribulation, that we may be able to comfort them which are in any trouble, by the comfort wherewith we ourselves are comforted of God" (KJV). His presence and constant watch and care are enough to sustain us.

**Listening**

Listening with an open heart and mind to the older adult's story is a powerful way to show them love and support. This also helps to build trust and a good relationship between the counselor and the older adults. James 1:19 says "Let every man be swift to hear, slow to speak, slow to wrath" (KJV). When we are in traumatic situations feelings lonely and cannot find the way out one should listen to the word of God. Acting on the word of God involves total embrace and surrender to His word, His will and His way. The key to listening is patience, gentleness, which will bring solace to the older adults in time of trouble. These, as guided by the Scriptures are key to listening in therapeutic relationships.

These biblical techniques can help older adults struggling with a traumatic crisis find peace and healing. Christian counselors can help older adults find hope and strength amid their struggles by providing spiritual guidance and support.

The biblical techniques for Christian counseling for older adults can be used to provide spiritual guidance and support in various situations. For example, when an older adult is dealing with the loss of a loved one, the counselor can use prayer and Bible study to help the individual find comfort and hope. Additionally, the counselor can use reflection and listening to help the older adult process their emotions and experiences. Furthermore, providing encouragement, confessing, and repenting of wrongdoings, forgiving those who have hurt them in the past, giving comfort and support, offering guidance, and affirming their worth and value can help the older adult find peace and healing.

Overall, the biblical techniques for Christian counseling for older adults can provide spiritual guidance and support to individuals struggling with a traumatic crisis. By utilizing the methods outlined in this book, counselors can help the older adult find hope and strength during their struggles.

## PART IV: BIBLICAL AND OTHER TECHNIQUES FOR CHRISTIAN COUNSELORS

Biblical techniques are based on the idea that spiritual and religious beliefs can be a foundation of strength and comfort during times of crisis. This approach focuses on helping people draw power and hope from their faith. It involves guiding the individual to discover and reflect on their faith and to find meaning and comfort in the Bible.

The counselor can also use prayer and meditation to help the person connect with God and find solace.

**Teachings of Jesus and the Bible**

The teachings of Jesus and the Bible can provide comfort and hope in times of distress. Jesus taught that God is always present and will never leave us, even in times of sorrow and suffering (Matthew 28:20). He also taught that we could find strength in our faith, even in the darkest of times (John 16:33). The Bible also provides many examples of God's presence and guidance in times of distress (Psalm 23; Isaiah 41:10). These teachings can give comfort and hope to those who are struggling with traumatic crisis and can help them to cope with their pain and suffering in a meaningful way.

**Case Study**

Mrs. Brown is an 85-year-old widow struggling with her husband's death. She is overwhelmed by grief and guilt and has difficulty coping with the changes in her life. To help Mrs. Brown, the counselor will use a combination of cognitive-behavioral techniques, biblical techniques, and spiritual care.

First, the counselor will help Mrs. Brown to identify and challenge her negative thoughts and beliefs. He can do this by encouraging her to think about the positive aspects of her life, such as her faith and relationships with family and friends. The counselor will also help Mrs. Brown to work through her grief and guilt by exploring how her faith can provide comfort and hope. He can do this by encouraging her to read the Bible, reflect on its teachings, pray, and meditate. Finally, the counselor will provide spiritual care by helping her to connect with a spiritual community and to draw strength from her faith.

To apply the approach to Christian counseling for older adults, the counselor must first assess the person's needs and develop a treatment plan tailored to their situation. The treatment plan should include a combination of cognitive-behavioral techniques, biblical techniques, and spiritual care. The counselor should also provide the person with emotional and practical support, as well as resources and referrals if needed.

For example, the counselor could use an approach using the following strategies to help Mrs. Brown cope with her grief and guilt:

Identify and challenge her negative thoughts and beliefs.

Explore how her faith can provide comfort and hope.

Encourage her to read the Bible and to reflect on its teachings.

Encourage her to pray and find solace in her faith.

Connect her with a spiritual community and help her to draw strength from her faith.

Provide her with emotional and practical support.

Provide her with resources and referrals, if needed.

When using biblical techniques in Christian counseling, it is essential to consider the needs of the client and the context in which the counseling is taking place. Biblical courses provide a helpful way to address the spiritual and emotional needs of older adults experiencing a traumatic crisis. As discussed in the volume edited by Geretic and Kennedy, the following are some commonly used biblically based techniques in Christian counseling for older adults.

*Proverbs* 12:25: This verse encourages older adults to seek wisdom and understanding, rather than to rely on their own knowledge. It can provide the necessary motivation and strength to seek the help and guidance of God in times of difficulty.

*Psalm 103:17-18:* This verse reminds older adults that God is their refuge and strength and that He is a basis of comfort and peace in times of crisis. It encourages them to turn to God for help and to trust Him in all circumstances.

*Romans 8:28*: This verse reassures older adults that God is in control and that He will work all things together for their good, no matter the circumstances they are facing. It encourages them to belief that God has a plan for them.

*Isaiah 43:2*: This verse reminds older adults that God is with them and will never leave them. It encourages them to find strength in knowing that God will never abandon them, no matter their circumstances.

Other biblical techniques for Christian counseling for older adults include spiritual direction, meditation, and journaling. Spiritual leadership involves discussing the individual's spiritual life and helping them to understand how their faith can help them cope with life's difficulties. Meditation is a practice of focusing on the present moment and connecting with God. Journaling is a practice of writing about one's thoughts and feelings and can help individuals process their experiences.

## Approaches to Christian Counseling for Older Adults: Use of Non-Religious Therapies

Christian counseling for older adults is an approach to helping individuals struggling with aging, trauma, and mental health issues. This type of counseling aims to provide support and guidance to individuals to help them live a more fulfilling and meaningful life. Christian counseling for older adults can take many forms, including individual, group, and family therapy.

It is to be noted that when a Christian counsellor views the range of what are mainly non-religious therapies, there is an intimidating array of options and they vary significantly as to whether they fit or do not with a Christian perspective.[2] In this section, I review three well-known counseling frameworks whose origins are not in biblical counseling nor are their origins or contemporary practices usually seen as connected to Biblical approaches. But they can be adapted to be part of the repertoire of such counseling so long as the counselor never loses sight of how their work needs to be guided by Christian teaching no matter what specific therapeutic approach is being utilized. The three approaches that are primarily non-religious in their origins are psychodynamic psychotherapy, cognitive behavioral therapy (CBT), and person-centered approaches.

### *Psychodynamic Theory*

Psychodynamic psychotherapy is generally seen as beginning with the ideas and techniques of Sigmund Freud. The psychodynamic approach to Christian counseling for older adults is based on the idea that unresolved conflicts from the past can harm the present. The approach and the broader field of psychotherapy of which it is part does not seem compatible with biblically based counselling. Its roots are in a very secular world view: "Psychoanalytic theory treats God as an illusion" (Got Questions, para. 7). For Freud, religion was at best a transitional tool in therapy, as one commentator put it, like a toy doll that gives superficial comfort in early healing! (Lamothe 437). More of a problem is that many psychotherapists look on religion as a crutch, and perhaps even as a major source of the counselees underlying troubles. My contention is that such a view neglects the diverse and positive ways in which the Scriptures hold the key to healing within a counselling relationship.

---

[2] Jones and Butman have thoroughly surveyed most commonly encountered psychotherapies from a Christian perspective.

In psychodynamic therapy, human behavior is seen to be driven by motives and instincts unknown to the individual her- or himself. The approach focuses on helping the person identify, understand, and work through these conflicts to gain insight into their current situation. The counselor can use a variety of techniques, such as free association, dream analysis, and interpretation of defense mechanisms, to help the person to gain insight into their unconscious thoughts and feelings. Speaking of what he calls spiritually oriented psychodynamic psychotherapy, Shafranske explains, "God images or other symbolic representations of the transcendent have the power to evoke emotions, which in turn, influence motivation and behavior . . . this therapeutic approach encourages the analysis of the functions religion and spirituality serve" (147).

Opening the path of healing that the psychodynamic approach creates can be readily related to passages in the Bible. Carson et al. discuss the unconscious by reviewing important scriptures that describe the workings and issues of what they call "the unconverted subconscious." (276). They provide a table connecting the concepts used in the psychodynamic approach. Of note are instances where The Psalmist in Psalm 51 and, later, the Apostle Paul acknowledge how they must wrestle to know deep and somewhat hidden parts of themselves. Psalm 51: "Behold thou desireth truth in the inward parts; and in the hidden part, thou shalt make me to know wisdom" KJV). And in 1 Romans 7:23, " But I see another law in my members [appetites and desires], warring against the law of my mind, and bringing me into captivity to the law of sin which is in my members.

In short, while the roots of psychodynamic therapy are more in ordinary science than in spirituality, the counselor can and should connect its insights to the far deeper roots of faith.

**Case Study:** Mrs. Brown is an 85-year-old widow struggling with her husband's death. She is overwhelmed by grief and guilt and has difficulty coping with the changes in her life. To help

Mrs. Brown, the counselor can use a combination of cognitive-behavioral techniques, biblical techniques, psychodynamic approaches, and spiritual care.

First, the counselor can help Mrs. Brown to identify and challenge her negative thoughts and beliefs through cognitive-behavioral techniques. He can do this by encouraging her to think about the positive aspects of her life, such as her faith and relationships with family and friends. Additionally, the counselor can use psychodynamic approaches to help Mrs. Brown to gain insight into her grief and guilt. He can do this by encouraging her to explore her feelings, reflect on her relationships with her husband and other loved ones, and identify any past unresolved conflicts that may be contributing to her current struggles.

The counselor can also use biblical techniques to help Mrs. Brown to draw strength and hope from her faith. He can do this by encouraging her to read the Bible, reflect on its teachings, pray, and meditate. Finally, the counselor can provide spiritual care by helping Mrs. Brown.

### Cognitive-Behavioral Techniques

Cognitive-behavioral techniques (CBT), unlike psychodynamic therapy, focus on the current problems that the client has and practical ways of confronting these. "The central premise of CBT is that thought patterns and beliefs, emotional state, and behavior are all interconnected . . . CBT emphasizes two effective ways to modify emotions. First is to identify, challenge, and change cognitive processes (i.e., how one views a situation), and second is to change behavior" (Pearce et al. 60) The counselee is guided as she or he  identifies and change negative thoughts and ideas that may perpetuate the traumatic crisis.

CBT was originated by Dr. Aaron T. Beck in the 1960s and was principally about cognitive distortions, the observation that "patients with depression often verbalized thoughts that were lacking in validity" (Chand et al. 2). Cognitive-behavioral counselors use a variety of specific methods to achieve these goals, such as:

Cognitive restructuring: This involves helping the person to identify and challenge unhelpful thoughts or beliefs.

Exposure therapy assists the person in confronting and coping with their fears or traumatic memories in a safe and controlled setting.

Relaxation techniques: This consists in helping the person to identify and practice relaxation strategies such as deep breathing and progressive muscle relaxation.

Skills training: This involves teaching the person how to manage emotions and cope with environmental stressors.

For Christian individuals with psychological issues, it stands to reason that among the key distorted underlying thought patterns, are ones that relate to their spiritual or religious orientation.[3] Thus, connecting to those beliefs—the underlying strategy of CBT— is important in two ways: surfacing whether the client understands the biblical wisdom that can help them deal with their issues and second, looking for what can be distorted and dysfunctional learnings that arose in the individual's religious upbringing. An example of the latter would be people who take from that background the idea of having to be perfect lest God rejects them. When that is happening, only a broader understanding of the scriptures can help the counselee appreciate the blessed act of forgiveness. Once such beliefs are brought out, the counselee can be referred to the Bible to confirm the importance of one's current thinking—Proverbs 23:7 says, "For as he thinks in his heart, so is he" (NKJV). This can be linked with the many passages of the Bible demonstrating the Lord's willingness to forgive. For example, there is Hebrews 8:12— "For I will be merciful to their unrighteousness, and their sins and their iniquities will I remember no more" (KJV)— and the well-

---

[3] Several studies have been done showing the usefulness of combining cognitive behavioral therapy with spiritually-guided counselling. See, for example Pearce et al., Pittman, and Turgut and Fusun

known story of how Joseph forgave the brothers who sold him into slavery (Genesis 50: 15–21). Thus, for the counselee for whom the Bible remains key to their understandings, the underlying premises of CBT are amenable. Accordingly, Pearce et al. have outlined several ways by which religious beliefs and CBT can be used together:

"Renewing of the mind" (61) which is synonymous with repenting;

"Scripture Memorization and Contemplative Prayer" (61) in which clients are assigned passages of the scriptures related to the problems they have identified and to then memorize these;

"Challenging Thoughts Using One's Religious Resources . . .What makes this different from conventional CBT is that a theological reflection for each style of thinking is provided and discussed" (61–62);

"Religious Practices" (62) in which actions are identified whereby behaviors can be modified to include forgiveness, gratitude . . . Praying for self and others" (62) etc.

Pearce et al. sum up by proposing what they refer to as religious cognitive behavior therapy (RCBT).

**Case Study: Surfacing Guilt and Finding Forgiveness (A).** Mr. Smith is an 80-year-old widower struggling with his wife's death. He married her for over 60 years, and they were both devoted Christians. He is suffering from feelings of loneliness and depression, as well as guilt for not being able to save her. He also has difficulty sleeping and finds himself overwhelmed with sadness and regret.

To help Mr. Smith, the counselor will use a combination of cognitive-behavioral techniques, biblical techniques, and spiritual care. First, the counselor will help Mr. Smith to identify and challenge his negative thoughts and beliefs. He can do this by encouraging him to think about the positive aspects of his life, such as his faith and relationships with family and friends. The counselor will also help Mr. Smith to work through his grief and guilt by exploring how his faith can provide comfort and hope. Finally, the counselor will provide spiritual care by helping him to connect with a spiritual community and to draw strength from his faith.

**Case Study 2: Surfacing Guilt and Finding Forgiveness (B).** Mrs. Jones is a 75-year-old widow struggling with her husband's recent death. She is overwhelmed by feelings of sadness and loss and a sense of being overwhelmed and confused by the many changes in her life. She is also struggling with guilt for not being able to save her husband.

To help Mrs. Jones, the counselor will use a combination of cognitive-behavioral techniques, biblical techniques, and spiritual care. First, the counselor will help Mrs. Jones to identify and challenge her negative thoughts and beliefs. He can do this by encouraging her to think about the positive aspects of her life, such as her faith and relationships with family and friends. The counselor will also help Mrs. Jones to work through her grief and guilt by exploring how her faith can provide comfort and hope. Finally, the counselor will provide spiritual care by helping her to connect with a spiritual community and to draw strength from her faith.

### *The Person-Centered Approach*

Of the three therapeutic approaches not generally seen as Christian in origin or practice, the person-centered approach (PCA) is, from my perspective, the one most amenable to spirituality. Carl Rogers is generally seen as the founder of PCA[4] who, from the outset, recognized spirituality as a potential resource in the struggle for healing. What distinguishes PCA from most other therapies, is that the client, not the counsellor plays the dominant role in identifying her or his

---

[4] Van Belle argues that "PCA has roots as far back as the Greeks and … resonates with basic themes found in the history of Western thought" (50)—including the Judaeo-Christion tradition.

underlying thoughts and issues. Rogers emphasized the potentially healing place of self-understanding and spirituality in the "inherent tendency of the organism to develop all its capacities . . . if self and experience are incongruence, then the general tendency to actualize . . . may work at cross purposes with the tendency to actualize the self (Rogers 196–197). This "incongruence" leads to maladjustment: in PCA, that is what the counselee must themselves lead in probing, discovery, and change.

In PCA, open discussion with the patient and their family that brings forth their spiritual views and encourages them to incorporate these int the management plan will benefit the patient and the team. A person-centered approach is key to ensuring that the patient's spirituality is understood *from their perspective*. The best health treatment will be strategies consistent with their spiritual or religious views. Van Belle says, "the Person- Centered Approach, fosters non-directivity and a receptive, listening attitude to life rather than one of manipulation. The Person-Centered Approach prizes life and other people as gifts to be received, and it counsels us to open up to one's own lived experience as a way of healing themselves." (52). Galatians 5:1 guides the counselee to recognize within themselves what Van Belle called "a free gift of grace" (52): "Stand fast therefore in the liberty wherewith Christ has made us free."

Figure 3 illustrates how to solve the problem of meeting the special needs of patients by healthcare professionals and services.

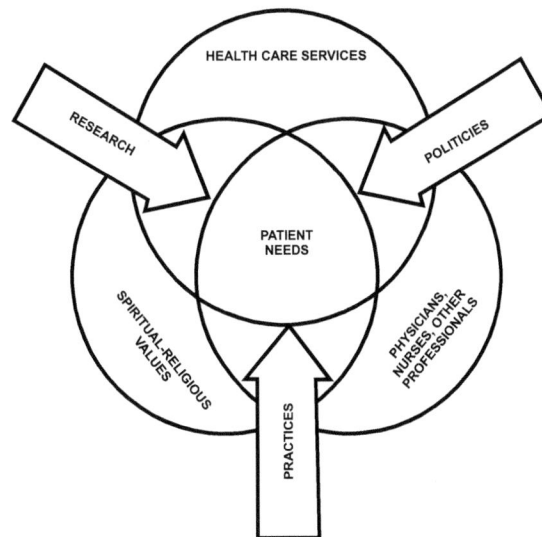

Fig. 3. Balancing the elements of attention to the unique needs of patients to empower resources on spiritual/religious coping.

The elements that are at stake are the institutions (health care and rehabilitation), the people associated with the process (physicians, nurses, other professionals), and the individual values of the patient (religious and spiritual). The forces that bind these elements are scientific research on the subject, the good practices adopted by institutions, and government policies that support these achievements.

**Conclusion**

Christian counseling for older adults is an approach to helping individuals struggling with aging, trauma, and mental health issues. This type of counseling can take many forms, including individual, group, and family therapy. Approaches to Christian counseling for older adults include those based on the teachings of Jesus and the Bible, but also, may be combined with such non-religious approaches as psychodynamic theory, and cognitive-behavioral techniques, and person-centered therapy. Biblical practices such as Bible study, prayer, spiritual direction, meditation, and journaling can help individuals understand and cope with their experiences. Through the counseling process, older adults can gain insight into their behavior and beliefs, identify sources of support and strength, and learn new ways of thinking and behaving that will help them cope with stress and difficult life situations.

## PART V: SPIRITUAL CARE FOR OLDER ADULTS EXPERIENCING TRAUMATIC CRISIS

Older adults often face various issues that can lead to traumatic crises. Understanding the impacts of aging, the physical and mental health complications that can arise, and the social factors that can contribute to the problem is essential.

Aging can cause physical and mental health issues due to the natural decline in bodily systems and organs. This can lead to decreased physical and psychological functioning, which can cause frustration, anger, and depression. Social factors can also contribute to the traumatic crisis, such as isolation, poverty, and the death of loved ones.

It is essential to recognize that older adults may have difficulty expressing their emotions or be unable to articulate the source of their distress fully. A counselor must create a safe, respectful, and supportive environment to help the client feel comfortable and heard. It is also essential to be aware of any cultural or religious differences that may be present.

Through compassionate listening and understanding, counselors can help older adults identify and express their feelings and provide them with the necessary resources and support to help manage the crisis. It is also essential to provide interventions tailored to the individual's needs, such as cognitive therapy, relaxation techniques, or resource referrals.

By understanding older adults' needs and providing interventions tailored to the individual, counselors can help clients navigate traumatic crises and find healing.

### Establishing a Safe, Respectful, and Supportive Environment

When counseling older adults experiencing a traumatic crisis, creating a safe, respectful, and supportive environment is essential, this can be done by actively listening to their story, validating their feelings and experiences, and providing them with reassurance and understanding.

It is also essential to know that older adults may need extra time and patience to process their emotions and thoughts.

It is also essential for the counselor to remain non-judgmental and use appropriate language for an older adult. This includes being mindful of the terms and avoiding slang or another language that may be unfamiliar to them. The counselor should also be aware of the older adult's cultural and religious background and should respect their beliefs and values when providing counseling.

It is also essential to provide a safe and supportive physical environment. The counselor should ensure that the office or room is clean, comfortable, and private. The background should be free from distractions and any potential triggers that may be present. The counselor should also be mindful of any mobility issues or other special needs of the older adult. This may include providing a chair or other furniture that is comfortable and easy to access.

Finally, it is crucial to provide emotional support and reassurance to the older adult. This can be done by encouraging them, reminding them they are not alone, and offering hope that things can get better. The counselor should also be aware of the potential for emotional triggers and provide a safe space for the older adult to express their feelings without fear of judgment or criticism.

## Link Between Spirituality and Religion

Religion is a source of spirituality for many people, but others discover their spirituality through other means, such as contact with the natural world, expression in the arts, the pursuit of scientific truth, or adherence to a code of ethics. Spiritual fulfillment is not contingent on religious affiliation. A person might be spiritually evolved outside from religious fervor. Of course, the opposite is also correct. People of varying religious persuasions and others whose beliefs don't neatly align with any established faith may find spirituality to be crucial. On the other hand, someone can be highly religious (often going to church) but spiritually undeveloped (not deeply experiencing these aspects). Even though they may not have any personal connection to spirituality, many people attend religious services regularly. Table 2 shows the primary ways in which these two ideas can be distinguished from one another.[5]

**Table 2**

*Primary Factors that Shape Religious and Spiritual Practices*

| RELIGION | SPIRITUALITY |
|---|---|
| A coherent body of doctrines. | Improvisational and varied; not doctrinal. |
| Culture plays a crucial role in determining. | Factors shared by all humans. |
| Locally based group with emphasis on helping the community (from outside to inside). | Personal, introspective reflection (from inside to outside). |
| Objective, quantifiable, and observable. | Having less objective evidence and measurement. |
| Strictly conventional; well-structured. | Relaxed in its approach, less dogmatic, and less methodical. |
| Behaviors that are oriented toward the outside world. | Subjective and introspective; emotions of calm and belonging |
| Behaving in a dictatorial fashion | Neither autocratic nor strictly accountable |
| Behaviors that are oriented toward the outside world | Behaviors based on inward-looking reflection, |

[5] Kennedy compares religion to spirituality in the context of counseling for the elderly,.

## Spiritual and Religious Coping

Making pain more manageable by providing purpose. When dealing with traumatic life events like loss or change, people often turn to spiritual-religious (S-R) coping strategies. Patients' reactions to disease, transition, and external factors beyond their control can be regulated by their religious beliefs and practices.[6]

Patients' capacity to deal with disease is affected by their spirituality. Comfort, a source of wisdom to make sense of the seemingly incomprehensible, and a ritualized means to confront the fundamental spiritual problems of meaning, value, and relationship are all things that many people find in their religious or spiritual beliefs and practices. Among the many facets of religious coping are:

The mental or cognitive side is how we interpret information. They consist of things like: "Why do bad things happen to good people?" "What happens after death?"

The importance of connection and personal strength are key to the experiences we have. Included in this category are inquiries like, "Do I exist independently, or am I part of something greater?" "Is there any reason to believe that things will improve?"

There are behavioral consequences of a person's spiritual beliefs and inner spiritual state, as these factors influence the individual's behavior and the choices that person makes in life. S-R factors may act as a direct mediator of the response to life stressors because they provide a cognitive framework for supplying meaning, so facilitating a more positive appraisal of those pressures. When faced with adversity, this may help you mentally bounce back faster. Religious traditions around the globe accord significance to the experience of pain, albeit they do so in widely divergent

---

[6] See Dein on "The Faith of Patients"

ways. As a result, it is not universally viewed as something to be avoided at all costs because it is harmful or embarrassing.[7]

Improvement in a wide range of subjects is one of spirituality's gifts. Hope, altruism, idealism, the meaning of life, and the acceptance of one's own suffering are all things he brings to his own relationship with himself (the intrapersonal realm). Tolerance, unity, and a feeling of belonging are gifts of the interpersonal sphere (with other people). Awakening feelings of unconditional love, devotion, and the conviction that one is not alone are hallmarks of the transpersonal realm (one with a superior power).

A person's spiritual beliefs can help them feel more in charge of their own lives by influencing how they process, react to, and ultimately make sense of the world around them. There is evidence from the past to suggest that people who have religious beliefs are better equipped to deal with stressful, out-of-their-control occurrences by reinterpreting and reframing them.

Having a reason to live is crucial. A loss of meaning like this is a major consequence of being ill. For both melancholy and spirituality, this loss and the subsequent process of rediscovery were crucial elements. Through the centrality of liturgy, worship, and prayer in the world's major religious traditions, spirituality may provide people a sense of direction in life. One's perspective on adversity may vary. Religion gives us a framework within which to make sense of hardship.[8]

Spirituality and religion, for example, are broad categories that can be interpreted in several ways. Negative S-R coping mechanisms do exist. The way people view and practice S-R rites can cut both ways. Even if there is evidence that religion has favorable effects on health as a whole, there is also the possibility that religious practice can have negative effects in some situations. It

---

[7] See Lindridge on the role of pain in recovery from mental health problems.
[8] See Anandarajah on the positive connections between undergoing hardship and religion.

does not appear that people's level of religious activity (such as church attendance) is particularly important in predicting health outcomes, but rather how they use their religious beliefs to weather difficult times. Some good and negative elements of S-R coping are presented in Table 3.

**Table 3**

*Some Aspects of Positive and Negative Coping of Spirituality and Religion*

| ISSUE | POSITIVE | NEGATIVE |
|---|---|---|
| What does it evoke? | Brings out the best in individuals, reinforcing active problem-solving behavior | Encourages negative avoidance strategies based on beliefs of abandonment and punishment |
| View of the deity | Faith in a kind, supportive God | Seeing God as distant and uncaring, or punishing for transgressions |
| Effect on life adjustments and emotional health | Lowers levels of psychiatric symptoms; linked with improved healthcare outcomes | Associated with a higher prevalence of psychiatric symptoms; worse medical outcomes |

**Effects of Spirituality-Religion on Health**

Health outcomes in the areas of cardiovascular disease, high blood pressure, stroke, immune system dysfunction, cancer, lifespan, pain, disability, and reduced use of health care services are all positively correlated with religious or spiritual practice. Increased religiosity is also correlated with a decrease in healthy lifestyle habits including regular exercise, cutting back on bad vices like smoking and alcohol, avoiding burnout, and strengthening bonds within the family. Greater religiosity is associated with a lower risk of developing and a quicker recovery from marital strife, depression, stress, suicide attempt, and substance misuse. The advantages usually come in three forms: helping with prevention, facilitating rehabilitation, and encouraging resilience in the face of health problems.

The methods by which spirituality may promote psychological health have been the subject of several investigations. Positive coping strategies have been shown to have a beneficial effect on mental health. Several physiological processes related to health may benefit from spiritual practices. A person's physical health may benefit from the spiritual pursuit of happiness, forgiveness, hope, and love. In addition, spirituality has been shown to lower levels of stress-inducing negative emotions including wrath, fear, and vengeance.

There is a wide range of ideas that attempt to account for the potential health benefits of S-R well-being. Possible explanations include an upbeat cognitive evaluation, a shift in mental state during prayer, and the support of a religious group.

Evaluation of knowledge: Religion is a source of optimism. In Christianity and Judaism, for instance, the existing condition of affairs will soon change with the arrival of a messianic period, regardless of how horrible things may seem on earth at the moment. Belief in an all-powerful God who provides comfort in times of trouble can be therapeutic. Indirect gains, such as easing the anxiety of dying among the elderly, may also increase as a result of religious belief. There may be positive outcomes from the tendency of religious people to focus on others rather than on themselves. Indeed, then, faith, hope, and optimism have numerous beneficial effects on health.

prayer: It is possible that the connection between the body, mind, and spirit, or even divine action, can be used to provide a biological explanation for the effects of some forms of prayer. The effects of prayer, like those of meditation, can be measured physiologically, with the heart rate dropping, brain waves shifting, and breathing rates decreasing. An individual's health may be positively affected by psychological mechanisms related to prayer, such as the relaxation response, improved social support, hope, and reduced distress. There are also spiritual considerations, such as the effect worship has on one's emotions. These mechanisms might also explain why praying for someone in their presence or with their knowledge is more effective.

The cultural impact of synagogue attendance involvement in a religious community provides inherently healthy circumstances for growing physical and mental health and can have a profound effect on a person's perspective on life, death, happiness, and suffering. Several factors have been linked to the lower rates of illness in religious communities, including a general emphasis on a healthy and sober way of life, protection from social isolation afforded by holy fellowship, strengthened family and community networks, a sense of belonging as well as self-esteem, and spiritual support in the face of adversity. People's mental health can often be improved via open dialogue with religious community members and leaders. Group participation in religious rituals has been associated with increased morality, self-respect, and a feeling of belonging.

## Spiritual Distress and Defensive Behaviors

In addition to their material bodies, human beings also have minds and souls. Discomfort can arise when any of these factors is compromised. Distress of a spiritual nature refers to an emotional state brought on by problems with one's beliefs or values. A mother, for instance, may have trouble reconciling the idea that God could allow her kid to perish while yet being loving. Patients may suffer from spiritual discomfort when they encounter existential suffering for which their faith offers no solace.

In the midst of their pain, patients feel exposed and mortal; their lives and the minds of their communities are shattered and broken. Therefore, one might gain access to his spirituality through the trials he faces. When the framework of beliefs is sound, it can be relied upon for solace, good fortune, safety, meaning, idealism, and even power. Beliefs are

Instead, negative emotions could be the result of a faulty belief system, which would be counterproductive to healthcare progress. Spiritual discomfort might increase if one's beliefs are shaken up. Several examples of possible expressions are shown below. used by many patients as a means of coping with their illnesses, and positive reinforcement can have an effect on the patient's recovery.[9]

*"Make a Deal with the Devil and Get Better"*—Parts of several texts where a deserving believer has his or her petition attended to give rise to the concept that one can negotiate with deities, spirits, saints, or even God to accomplish a specific conclusion. This kind of conduct is common among patients, especially those dealing with potentially fatal illnesses. While it is great when this outlook improves a patient's outlook, it can become problematic when it causes them to overestimate their chances of recovery and hinders their treatment.

*The fatalist karma idea— "Bad things happen to them because they deserve it."* This can place a person in a "sell-out" position, where they confuse submitting to God's will with giving up on life. The patient's decisions may be guided by negative values even if they don't seem to care.

*Loss of meaning or purpose (demotivation).* These are essential in life. A loss of meaning like this is a major consequence of being ill. For both melancholy and spirituality, this loss and the subsequent process of rediscovery were crucial elements. Through the centrality of liturgy, worship, as prayer in the world's major religious traditions, spirituality may provide people a sense of direction in life. A spiritual representation of the patient's condition is the fight for renewed or continued purpose in life. Religion gives people faith in a better future. A person's spiritual beliefs may help them feel more in charge of their own lives by improving their capacity to process, adapt to, and make sense of the world around them. Reframing or reinterpreting events, which may lead to new meaning and insight, is not an option for people with a dysfunctional religious belief system who are reacting to things they see as beyond their control.

---

[9] See Dunn's. "Psych-Wise Guide to Navigating Social Life."

*Disruption brought on by shame, confusion.* Religions that emphasize shame, like Orthodox Judaism and Catholicism, can have negative psychological effects. Walking in circles paralyzed by a constellation of confusing emotions, is a waste of time and energy. Certain religious believers may mistakenly believe that you should either (a) not take pain medication at all or (b) not take enough pain medication because they fear you will become addicted; (b) pain should be dealt with only spiritually and that taking medication for pain relief is relying on anything other than God; (c) pain should not be reassured because it results in spiritual growth; and (d) if you still have pain, then your faith is not strong enough.

*Sorrow, Betrayal, Angry to God (Disappointment).* The idea of a supportive God with you in your suffering, the omnipotent God who supports a person through a crisis, can be psychologically beneficial. This concept is sometimes linked to the idea of a reward due to past good actions. A negative feeling of abandonment may surge when a person's prayer is not attended to.[10]

*Subtle Perception of Vulnerable and Finitude (Fear).* When patients suffer, they perceive a sense of their vulnerability & finitude, as well as a disturbance and fracture of their person and mind within the community. Emotional equilibrium can be disrupted by the worry of losing something important (a physical ability, autonomy, or even one's life).

The patient's clinical therapy and quality of life may be negatively impacted by the patient's subsequent defensive behaviors caused by spiritual distress. Some examples of such behaviors are shown below.

*Believe in the All-Powerful Nature of Religion without Questioning Its Veracity.* Stronger coping mechanisms would be developed with the help of religion. As part of a broader management

---

[10] This is discussed by Menkel-Meadow in "Critical Moments Reconsidered."

strategy, religious practice can have positive effects on mental health and decrease emotional discomfort. As opposed to the coping strategies based on delaying (where the individual waits for God to intervene on their behalf). The prognosis of psychiatric diseases may be worsened by an individual's over-reliance on religious rituals or prayer. Strict dedication to a "religious concept" may lead to suicide in extreme cases, such as those seen in very unusual new religious movements. For instance, "When the Lord wants to take me, He'll get me whatever I do" is a negative coping thinking as is the fateful corollary, "No need to go out and buy a ton of medicine that I may not need."

Unprecedented religious movements may emerge at times of great upheaval and unpredictability because religious fervor and sectarianism tend to intensify in the face of personal stress. People going through stressful life or health changes are more prone to become involved in alternative religion movements led by charismatic leaders. Only if it's not an attempt to avoid dealing with one's problems should one seek spiritual practices again.

Long-term participation in a religious group has been linked to an increased propensity to rely on guidance from religious leaders. A patient's right to seek counsel from a religious leader before making decisions concerning their health should not be questioned. Delegating authority to an outside body that only represents the religious perspective is risky.

*Symptoms of Ritualistic Obsession.* Formal religious organization, such as religious rituals and religiously based moral or ethical reasoning, can be seen as manifestations of the human cognitive capacity to order experience and seek meaning. This inclination is also a commendable and important human quality. Clinical excesses exist, however, in the ordering and attribution of meaning or significance to experience, just as they do in the attachment dimension. OCD risk may be higher in people who practice religions like Islam and Judaism, which place a premium on rituals. Therapeutic interventions that encourage regulation and containment may be necessary for some pathologic manifestations of desperate attachment behavior. Avoiding chaos in all areas of their lives, including their religious ones, requires therapeutic activity urging containment of the face of such attachment requirements. Overemphasis on imposing order through religious belief might cause rituals to become devoid of meaning.

*Sectarianism, Isolation, Fanaticism.* Any devastating effects can be elicited by the dominance of fanatic beliefs and consequent up-rootedness from the instinctive foundation. Excessive devotion to religious practices might result in family break-up if one spouse's sole preoccupation is with spiritual practice. Differences in the levels of religiosity between spouses may result in marital disharmony. Religion can promote rigid thinking, overdependence on laws and rules, an emphasis on guilt and sin, and disregard for personal individuality and autonomy.

*Refusal of Certain Treatments.* Clinical decisions may be affected by the patient's belief system when particular preconceptions interfere with healthcare. A person's religious beliefs may be the source of problematic concepts, spiritual stigmas, and stress that undermine treatment compliance. A person's religious beliefs may affect how open they are to trying new methods of treatment and setting new, more idealistic goals for their recovery. Koenig identifies four common misunderstandings about pain treatment held by people with strong religious beliefs: The patient may be unwilling to take pain medication (or may not take enough medication) for several reasons: (1) fear of becoming addicted to the medication; (2) the belief that pain should be handled with only in spiritual terms; (3) the belief that pain should not be reassured because pain may result in spiritual growth; (4) the belief that the patient's faith is not strong enough if they continue to experience pain.

**Outreach Care Programs and Other Activities**

*Group Process Outreach Program*

The Group Process Outreach Program is a group-based approach to helping older adults who are experiencing a traumatic crisis. This program involves visiting nursing homes, private homes, and other places of residence to provide support and encouragement to those in need. In this program, the counselor is responsible for leading a group of people through a series of activities and discussions designed to help them cope with the traumatic event. For example, a group process outreach program could involve visiting a nursing home and leading discussion groups on topics such as dealing with grief, facing the future, and building resilience.

Dr. Timothy Clinton suggests several specific activities for group process outreach programs. These include providing support groups, educational seminars, and other activities that encourage socialization and community building. The activities should be tailored to the needs of the participants and may include:

- Discussion groups that focus on topics such as grief, stress, and depression.

- Exercise classes that promote physical activity and mental health.

- Social activities such as board games, crafts, and other activities that foster connection and engagement.

- Music and art therapy that can help express and process emotions.

Finally, the group process outreach program provides Christian counselors with the opportunity to observe older adults in their natural environment. This can be a valuable tool for assessing their needs and providing them with the help and resources they need to cope with their situation. Overall, the group process outreach program outlined in Competent Christian Counseling is a valuable tool for helping older adults experiencing traumatic crisis. By visiting nursing homes, private homes, and other places of residence, Christian counselors can provide the support and resources needed to help older adults cope with their situation. Additionally, organized activities and informal opportunities to connect with others can help older adults to develop meaningful relationships and find comfort in their faith. Finally, observing older adults in their natural environment provides Christian counselors with the opportunity to assess their needs and provide them with the help they need.

*Stress Management:*

Stress is a natural response to traumatic events, and older adults may be particularly vulnerable to its effects. As a Christian counselor, you can help older adults develop and utilize stress management strategies. These might include relaxation techniques, exercise, and other forms of self-care. For example, helping an older adult to practice stress management techniques such as deep breathing, progressive muscle relaxation, and mindfulness.

Case Study: Dr. Timothy is a Christian counselor who works with older adults experiencing traumatic crisis. He recently worked with an 82-year-old woman who had just been diagnosed with a terminal illness. She was struggling with depression and anxiety due to her diagnosis and was feeling overwhelmed. Dr. Timothy first focused on providing the woman with a safe and supportive space to express her feelings. He then focused on helping her develop stress management strategies. He encouraged her to take time to practice relaxation techniques and to engage in regular physical activity. Dr. Timothy also reminded her of Bible examples that could provide her with hope and comfort during this difficult time.

Finally, Dr. Timothy encouraged her to reach out to her family and friends for support. He also helped her to find local support groups for older adults going through similar experiences. Through his counseling and support, the woman was able to find a sense of peace and comfort during her crisis.

*Using the Bible to Cope with Difficulty*

This topic is in many ways the most central to what it is to be a Christian or biblically based counselor to the elderly. In Dr. Timothy Clinton's case study on *Using Bible Examples to Help Older Adults Experiencing Traumatic Crisis.*patients was an elderly woman who had recently experienced the death of her husband, who had been her life partner for over 60 years. The woman was grieving heavily and struggling to come to terms with the loss.

Dr. Clinton used Bible examples to help her find comfort in her difficult situation. He pointed out how Jesus wept at the death of his friend Lazarus, showing that it is natural to be sad and to feel sorrow for a loved one who has passed away. He also spoke about how Jesus rose from the grave, giving her hope in the knowledge that her husband, too, could be resurrected. Dr. Clinton also used Bible examples to show the woman that God was with her in her time of sorrow. He shared the story of Jesus calming the storm, showing her that even when life becomes chaotic and overwhelming, God is always present. He also spoke about how God has good plans for us, even in our darkest moments, and that He can use difficult times in our lives to bring about something positive.

In the book of Job, we read about a man who endured immense suffering and pain in his life. God allowed Satan to bring trials and tribulations upon Job, but God also remained with him throughout it all. Job's faith and trust in God remained unwavering, even in his darkest hour.

This story can be used to illustrate to older adults how God can bring good out of difficult situations. It can also be used to remind them that they are not alone in their struggles and that, no matter how bad things may seem, they can always turn to God for comfort and guidance. Even when it feels like the world is crumbling around them, Job's story can be a reminder that God is still with them, and that He has a plan for them even in the midst of suffering. It can also be a reminder that, no matter how difficult things may seem, God will never give them anything more than they can handle.

Overall, Dr. Clinton was able to provide comfort and encouragement to the woman in her time of grief, allowing her to move forward with hope and faith in the midst of her traumatic crisis.

*When a Client Is in Isolation*

Case Study: The following is a case study of an older adult experiencing isolation during a traumatic crisis. Mrs. Jones is an elderly woman who recently suffered a stroke. Due to the stroke, she was unable to leave her home and was forced to remain isolated from her family and friends. She was feeling lonely and afraid, and her family was unable to provide her with the support she needed.

As her Christian counselor, I visited Mrs. Jones in her home and provided her with a listening ear. I encouraged her to reach out to her family and friends, and offered her advice on how to stay connected even while she was confined to her home. I also shared Bible verses that spoke of God's comfort and presence in times of difficulty.

In addition, I provided Mrs. Jones with resources to help her stay connected to her community. I pointed her towards online support groups, home visits from volunteers, and other resources that could help her stay connected to others even while she was isolated. Through our sessions, Mrs. Jones was able to feel less alone and more connected to her family and community. She was also able to find comfort in God's presence and to trust that He would bring good out of her difficult situation.

When a client is in isolation, it is important to encourage them to maintain contact with family, friends, and other support networks. This can be done by encouraging them to participate in social activities such as church groups, support groups, and other activities that provide a sense of belonging. These activities can help to restore a sense of purpose and connection, which can help to reduce feelings of isolation. Additionally, it is important to provide a listening ear and offer support to the client, so that they know they are not alone in their struggles.

*When a Client Is Angry or Depressed:*

Dr. Timothy Clinton, President of the American Association of Christian Counselors, shared a case study of a man in his seventies who had been dealing with depression and anger. After offering prayer and listening to the man's story, Dr. Clinton realized that the man's anger and depression were rooted in a belief that he had failed in his marriage and family life. He was filled with regret and was consumed with guilt and shame over his past decisions and mistakes.

To help him, Dr. Clinton used Biblical examples of God's love and grace to remind the man that God had forgiven him and could still use his life for good. He also helped him work through the emotions of guilt and shame and encouraged him to forgive himself and move forward with a new perspective. Through prayer and counseling, the man was eventually able to accept God's forgiveness and recognize that he could still make a positive difference in the lives of those around him.

The Bible story of Joseph is an excellent example of how God can use difficult circumstances for good. Joseph was betrayed by his brothers, sold into slavery, and was wrongly accused of a crime he did not commit. Despite these hardships, Joseph was able to remain faithful to God and eventually was able to use his experiences to help save his family. This story can be used to remind older adults that even in difficult times, God is with them and can use even the most difficult circumstances for good.

In addition, it is important to remind older adults that seeking professional help is not a sign of weakness or failure, but rather it is a sign of strength and courage. Encourage them to seek help if needed and remind them that they are not alone in their struggles.

The case study demonstrates how Christian counseling can be effective in helping older adults who are struggling with anger and depression. Through prayer and counseling, the man was able to recognize his worth and the potential he had to make a difference in the lives of others.

*Inspirational Scriptures*

When a client is angry or depressed, it is important to emphasize that God is in control and that they can find strength in Him. Reminding them of the promises in scripture, such as "The fear of man bringeth a snare: but whoso putteth his trustin the Lord shall be safe" (Proverbs 29:25, KJV) can help them to remember that God is a source of comfort and hope even in the midst of difficult situations. Additionally, encouraging them to practice self-care, such as engaging in calming activities or spending time in nature, can help them cope with their emotions. Christian counseling can be an invaluable resource for older adults experiencing traumatic events. By utilizing group process outreach programs, providing stress management strategies, and using Bible examples, you can help them to cope with their emotions and find hope in God.

## PART VI: CASE STUDIES

In Part VI, an array of brief case accounts is presented showing both the variation in how counselees suffer and may be comforted with the Scriptures but also the similarities of their troubling situations. The problems faced by these older people overlap. The names are pseudonyms.

### Case 1—Eleanor: Lack of a Sense of Purpose/Motivation

Eleanor is a 79-year-old woman struggling with a lack of purpose and motivation in her life for the past few years. She is a widow, and her children are grown and living away from home. She has always been a very active member of her church and community, but now she feels like she has nothing to do and no one to turn to. She is looking for a way to find sense and purpose in her life again.

Several counseling goals are important in this case:

1. To help Eleanor identify her values and beliefs to develop a sense of purpose.

2. To help Eleanor understand the importance of maintaining physical and mental health to feel more energized and motivated.

3. To provide Eleanor with resources and support to help her regain a meaning of purpose and meaning in her life.

4. To encourage Eleanor to engage in meaningful activities that will bring joy and fulfillment to her life.

The counseling approach for Eleanor comprises these elements:

1. Utilize a person-centered approach to promote self-exploration. This will allow Eleanor to explore her own values, beliefs, and motivations to gain a better understanding of her purpose in life.

2. Utilize a strengths-based approach to build on Eleanor's current strengths and resources. This will help her to identify areas of growth and potential.

3. Utilize spiritual counseling techniques to help Eleanor explore her faith and religious beliefs. This will provide her with a sense of comfort and peace.

4. Utilize an integrative approach to counseling, combining elements of cognitive-behavioral therapy, positive psychology, and mindfulness-based interventions. This will enable Eleanor to identify and challenge any opposing thoughts or beliefs hindering her progress.

Many verses from the scriptures bolster these efforts, showing how important it is to know oneself. For example, in 1 Timothy 4:16, we are told, "Take heed unto thyself . . . for in doing this thou shalt save thyself and them that hear thee" (KJV). Or, in Probverbs 20:5, it is sai, "Counsel in the heart of man is like deep water; but a man of understanding will draw it out."

**Case 2—John: Coping with a Traumatic Event**

John is an 82-year-old widower living alone for the past five years. Recently, he experienced a traumatic event when his home was broken into, and his valuables were stolen. He struggles to cope with the event's aftermath and is feeling scared and anxious.

Biblical counseling is a practical approach to helping older adults struggling with traumatic events. This approach focuses on helping the individual find healing and comfort through the teachings of the Bible. Regarding the specific source of trauma, John should be reminded, for example, of Psalm 119: 61–62: "The bands of the wicked have robbed me: but I have not forgotten thy law. At midnight I will rise to give thanks unto thee" (KJV). Using Bible scriptures, the therapist can provide reassurance, comfort, and hope to the individual. Furthermore, the therapist can use cognitive behavioral therapy to help individuals reframe their thoughts and develop healthier coping strategies. By combining both biblical and cognitive behavioral approaches, the therapist can provide a holistic approach to helping the individual find peace and healing.

The therapy this case would focus on helping John process his traumatic experience and find healing in the relief of God's grace and love. The therapist can use scriptures from the Bible to encourage John, such as Psalm 34:18, which states, "The Lord is near to the brokenhearted and saves the crushed in spirit." The therapist can also help John develop a sense of safety and security by instilling in him the knowledge that God is always with him and that nothing can isolate him from the love of God. Furthermore, the therapist can use Cognitive Behavioral Therapy to help John cope with his anxiety and fears by teaching him relaxation techniques and allowing him to reframe his thoughts in a more positive light.

## Case 3—Mary: Struggling with Depression and Anxiety After Loss

Mary is a 76-year-old woman who is struggling with depression and anxiety. She recently lost her husband of 50 years and is having difficulty coping with her grief. Biblical counseling is a practical approach to helping older adults who are experiencing a traumatic crisis. The Bible is filled with stories of hope and healing for those aggrieved and these can provide comfort and peace through difficult times. Many of these are often spoken at funerals and memorial services yet can be revisited in the extended time after loss (all KJV):

Matthew 5:4 "Blessed are they that mourn: for they shall be comforted."

John 16:22: "And ye now therefore have sorrow: but I will see you again, and your heart shall rejoice, and your joy no man taketh from you."

Revelation 21:4 "And God shall wipe away all tears from their eyes, and there shall be no more death, neither sorrow, nor crying."

Biblical counseling can help older adults find strength in God's love and grace and provide them with the tools and resources they need to cope with their situation. Furthermore, the use of

CBT can help older adults to reframe their thoughts and worries in a more positive light and can help them to develop healthy coping skills that can be used in the future.

In this case, biblical treatment would focus on helping Mary find healing in God's love and grace. The therapist can use scriptures from the Bible to encourage Mary, such as Psalm 147:3, which states, "He heals the brokenhearted and binds up their wounds." The therapist can also help Mary develop a sense of peace and comfort by instilling in her the knowledge that God will never leave her side and will always be there for her in her time of need. Furthermore, the therapist can use CBT to help Mary cope with her depression and anxiety by teaching her relaxation techniques and allowing her to reframe her thoughts in a more positive light.

### Case 4—Joseph: Facing Loneliness and Depression

Joseph is an 84-year-old man who is struggling with loneliness and isolation. He recently moved to a new city and did not have any family or friends in the area. Crewdson has described the incidence of loneliness as a worldwide phenomenon. It is a certainty that the Christian counsellor will find that even when other psychological issues are prominent, the absence of those who the counselee loves and needs is a chronic underlying factor.

In this case, biblical treatment would focus on helping Joseph find a sense of community and companionship in God. The therapist can use scriptures from the Bible to encourage Joseph, such as Psalm 68:6 which states, "God setteth the solitary in families" (KJV). One therapeutic strategy is to help those who once were surrounded by family and friends to turn more to God. The therapist in this case can help Joseph develop a sense of belonging and connection by instilling in him the knowledge that God is always with him and will never leave him. Joshua 1:5 points out that we cannot expect to have those we love or are friends with around us all our lives: "There shall not any man be able to stand before thee all the days of thy life: as I was with Moses, so I will be with thee: I will not fail thee, nor forsake thee" (KJV). The therapist can use CBT and/or PCA to help Joseph cope with his loneliness by teaching him how to build relationships and make meaningful connections with others. Walker et al. survey an array of biblically based and other helps that counselors of lonely, elderly people can turn to.

**Case 5—Sara: Dealing with Chronic Pain**

Sara is a 73-year-old woman who is struggling with chronic pain. She has been dealing with this pain for many years and is finding it increasingly difficult to cope.

Therapy: In this case, biblical treatment would focus on helping Sara find healing in God's grace and love. The therapist can use scriptures from the Bible to encourage Sara, such as Psalm 34:17 which states "The Lord hears the prayer of the afflicted." The therapist can also help Sara develop a sense of hope and resilience by instilling in her the knowledge that God is always with her and will never leave her in her time of need. Furthermore, the therapist can use Cognitive Behavioral Therapy to help Sara cope with her pain by teaching her relaxation techniques and allowing her to reframe her thoughts in a more positive light.

**Case 6—James: Facing the Loss of Faith**

James is an 81-year-old man who is struggling with spiritual confusion and doubt. He is questioning his faith and is feeling lost and confused. His situation is far from unique as those who have live in hardship and sorrow are. Like Job in the Scriptures in a quandary of needing but doubting God.

In this case, biblical treatment would focus on helping James find clarity and understanding in his faith. The therapist can use scriptures from the Bible to remind James that tribulation is widespread seen in the sufferings of Job and Jonah. The story of Job is a vast and sometimes challenging study of a good and well-to-do man, brought low and, at first, angry with God for that suffering. Job days, Let the day perish wherein I was born . . . let that day be Darkness, let not God regard it from above." For the counselee like James who is in the grip of despair, the thought that

Job basically curses his birth unfortunately will resonate but then with time and in prayerful dialogue with God, Job comes to a different perspective: "Therefore have I uttered that I understood not; things too wonderful for me that I know not" (Job 42: 3). And Jonah says, "The waters compassed me about even to the soul; the depths closed me round about, the weeds were wrapped about my head" (Jonah 2: 5). And yet, "When my soul fainted within me, I remembered the Lord and my prayer came in unto thee. (Jonah 2:7).

In Jeremiah, God reassures: "For I know the thoughts that I think toward you, saith the Lord, thoughts of peace, and not of evil" (Jeremiah 29: 11). Such scriptures can have an enormous and positive impact on a person like James. From such passages, the therapist can also help James develop a sense of peace and comfort by instilling the knowledge that God is always with him and will never leave him. Furthermore, the therapist can use CBT to help James cope with his spiritual confusion and doubt by teaching him how to interpret scriptures and allowing him to reframe his thoughts in a more positive light.

### Case 7: Lawrence—Coping with the Aftermath of Trauma.

Lawrence is an older man who has recently experienced a traumatic event. He has been struggling to cope with the traumatic event's aftermath and has difficulty finding the strength to move forward. His faith in God has been shaken, and he wonders if his life will ever be the same. To help Lawrence, the counselor should first use Proverbs 12:25 to remind him that the Lord is his strength. The counselor should then focus on assisting Lawrence in building a relationship with God so that he can find solace in Him. The counselor can also use Psalm 103:17 to remind James that God will not forsake him, no matter what happens: But the mercy of the Lord is from everlasting to everlasting upon them that fear him The counselor should also encourage Lawrence to take practical steps to move forward, such as seeking joining a support group for the traumatized.

## PART VII: A TOOLKIT FOR PASTORAL COUNSELING

This part of the guide overviews a diverse array of activities—mainly accompanied by relevant prayers that I have used—which are instrumental in counseling the elderly. In all, the array is numerous, which reflects the need. Christian counsellors must have a broad and adaptable toolkit when seeking to help elderly clients because the situations, contexts, and needs are so manifold. This, this long section brings together such a toolkit. I have organized it into five categories which do overlap. Table 4 summarizes that organization and provides page numbers for where the subject is dealt with. The categories are:

1. Substantive Challenges Faced by the Client

2. Theoretical Bases of Counselling

3. Specific Techniques of Intervention

4. Biblically Based Counselling Methods

5. Other Skills for the Christian Counsellor

As noted, in many though not all sections of this toolkit, usually I provide a prayer that I have found helpful in tackling each challenge. These are highlighted in gold color.

**Table 4**

*Index for The Toolkit for Pastoral Counseling*

*1. SUBSTANTIVE CHALLENGES FACED BY THE CLIENT*     63

*Going Through Tough Times*   63

*Helping with Loss and Grief*   64

*Feeling Lonely: The Need for Prayer* 65

*Prayer Amidst Anger*   66

*Ensuring Safety and Achieving Security*     67

*Facing Traumatic Events*     69

*Maintaining One's Autonomy* 71

*Helping to Deal with Physical Pain   72*

*Coping with Family Issues—Interventions    74*

*Dealing with Social Isolation 74*

*Doing Forgiveness     76*

*2. THEORETICAL BASES OF COUNSELLING       77*

*Practicing Emotional Intelligence     77*

*Expanding One's Horizon: The Hermeneutic View   79*

*Applying Theories of Human Trauma 80*

*Exposure Therapy     82*

*Using Talk Therapy   83*

*Adlerian Theory: Encouragement     84*

*Solution-Focused Brief Therapy       86*

*Using Operant Conditioning for Counselee Adaptability     88*

*Moving Towards Mindfulness 89*

*3. SPECIFIC TECHNIQUES OF INTERVENTION 90*

 *Music Therapy: Using Music to Build Faith and Courage  90*

 *Using Talk Therapy   91*

 *Building Resilience   92*

 *Shifting to Positivity  93*

 *Empathetic Guidance         94*

 *Monitoring and Enhancing Physical Well-Being     96*

 *Monitoring and Managing Emotional Health       97*

 *Encouraging Activities that Increase Self Esteem     98*

 *Engaging with One's Community     99*

 *Bringing Out Accomplishments as a Counseling Technique 101*

 *Drawing on Recurring Themes       102*

 *House Calls: Visiting and Encouraging Fellowship With Other Older People      103*

*4. BIBLICALLY-BASED COUNSELLING TECHNIQUES   104*

*Building A Case for the Bible 104*

*Pastoral Talk  105*

*Developing Good Listening Skills: Pastoral Listening 106*

*5. SPECIFIC SKILLS FOR COUNSELLING PRACTICE    108*

*Thankfulness for Being Able to Counsel 108*

*Assigning Client Homework    109*

*Achieving Selflessness110*

*Praying with the Counselee    111*

*Viewing Our Lives with God's Perspective    113*

*Developing Problem-Solving Skills    114*

*Performance Evaluation        115*

*Supervision    116*

*Consultation with Other Christian Counselors        117*

*Reviewing Counselee Well-Being Outcomes  118*

*Using Available Data to Develop Best Counseling Practices        120*

*Enabling Counselees to Reflect on their Pastoral Counseling Practices    121*

*Developing Decision-Making Skills. 122*

*Arranging Conferences and Meetings    123*

## 1. Substantive Challenges Faced by the Client

This section is about the actual problems that older people face as well as prayers and some counselling strategies for helping them deal with these.

### *Going Through Tough Times*

When older adults experience traumatic events, they go through difficult times, and pastors can play a significant role in helping them navigate these tough times in their lives. Traumatic crisis causes emotional, physical, psychological, and spiritual harm, especially to older adults. Traumatic crises involve events such as natural disasters, deaths, sexual assault and abuse, violent crime, domestic violence, the aftermath of suicide, or threats to public health. However, in these situations where elderly people will feel overwhelmed or trapped, pastors are supposed to counsel them to absolutely trust in God and ask for His grace to go about their present situations.

It is not easy to make older adults consider the efficacy of prayers in the midst of these difficult situations. Still, this is feasible with commitment and praying for God's guidance. Pastors and priests are called to shepherd the believers. Looking after the believers is largely about being considerate of their well-being. Thus, with the help of God, servants of God (pastors and priests) will direct elderly people facing traumatic events on how to pray, to get strength and comfort through tough times.

### Prayer for Going Through Tough Times

*Dear Heavenly Father, I thank you for the life you have given me. I thank you because everything happens to us for a reason, and you always give us strength to overcome the challenges and temptations that come our way. I know you are aware of my current difficult situation, and without your strength, I will not make it. I honor you because your word says that you will never forsake me. I call upon you for your strength because the world around me is full of chaos, and I cannot find peace, and I feel overwhelmed. Take control of my life, for I solely rely on you. Dear Lord, I take hold and believe in your word in Galatians 5:1, which says, "It is for freedom that Christ has set you free." I am free of the stress and burdens of life in the bondage-breaking name of Jesus Christ. Amen.*

### Helping with Loss and Grief

For older people who lose loved ones, this worsens te sense of loneliness of not having anyone to turn to. Here the counselor can stand ion for the lost one and work to ensure that grieving eventually means relying more on God and His teachings. Effective advice for persons dealing with death can be given by biblical counselors who comprehend traumatic occurrences generally and who have taken into account biblical teaching on memories. The counselor will give examples of genuine traumatic occurrences, give a general overview of how the world views such events, and then suggest a framework for how Christians might successfully minister to persons who have been affected by trauma. Fig. 13 presents a visual model of therapy directed at grief and loss.

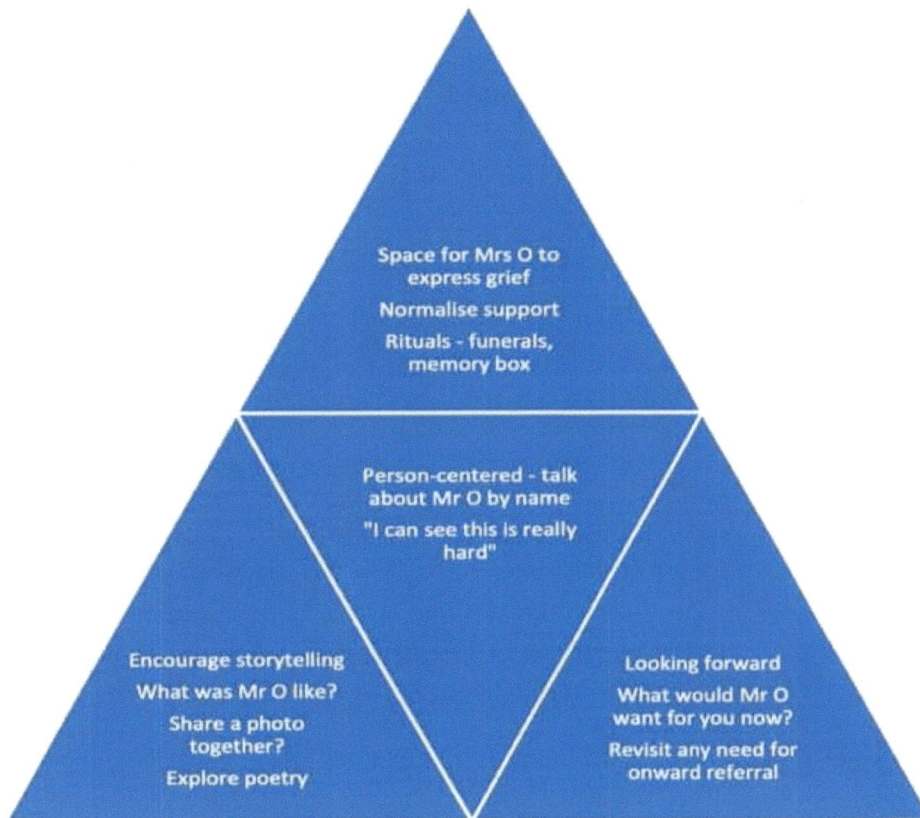

Fig. 13. A Model of Counseling for Grief and Loss.

Loss always produces grief. There is no escaping it. If you try to deny it or postpone it, it will only gather force and become more debilitating the longer you try to suppress it. That is one reason prayer is an indispensable resource for a grieving heart.

### *Prayer on Grief and Loss*

*Jesus, you said, "Blessed are those who mourn, for they will be comforted." (Matthew 5:4, NIV). I'm grieving; send me Your solace now. Fold Your arms around me and hold me tight. Send holy messengers of kindness to me. Shower Your solace on me through people around me and keep a long way from me those whose words and activities are no solace. In Jesus' name. Amen.*

### *Feeling Lonely: The Need for Prayer*

When people feel lonely, it develops because there are few available people to communicate with and to rely on when faced with dire situations. As people get older, the feeling of loneliness tends to creep, which is highly motivated by traumatic events. For instance, when an older adult loses their spouse, this feeling becomes more pronounced such that when the right action is not taken, these people could end up losing the taste for life. Our God wants his children to live their lives to the fullest. Considerably, it is written in John 10:10; "I have come to in order that you may have life—life in all its fullest" (RSV). Therefore, the servants of God should act to ensure their children of God live according to God's will.

The church could be visiting the elderly people at their homes; however, this may not fully make these people feel cared for and engaged. Thus, when are helped to develop the ability to overcome loneliness from within will be better than creating an external environment to address this issue. The story of Job gives us invaluable insights into how to stick with God in difficult situations. Job is a good example of a person who went through traumatic events and lost his family and wealth. Despite his loss, he kept faith and trust in God. Thus, elderly people can always be counseled to stay in God's presence, where they can find solace, company, and comfort in difficult moments in life. Thus, through prayer, this feeling can be overcome.

### Prayer When Lonely

*Dear God, I bless and adore you for the faith that you authored in me. Your word tells me that you are the author and finisher of my faith (Hebrews 12:2). I need your comfort, and I want to feel your presence because I feel lonely. During your birth here on earth, Jesus Christ, it was prophesied that you would be called Emmanuel, which means God with us. Dear Lord Jesus, feel the emptiness that I feel in my life. And help me understand that I will witness your marvelous works for your glory through this situation. In Jesus' name, Amen.*

### Prayer Amidst Anger

In their *Popular Encyclopedia of Christian Counseling* Clinton and Hawkins explain how demanding it is when caring for older adults with responsive (angry) behavior. This behavior can be triggered or developed by dementia or traumatic experiences. Responsive behavior may involve physical and verbal outbursts. In Christian teaching, this behavior is not condoned because 1 Corinthians 10:31 says, "So whether you eat or drink or whatever you do, do it all for the glory of God" (NIV). Despite being set free, Christians are advised by Apostle Paul to refrain from everything that may not glorify God. Apparently, abusive, or vulgar language will never please God; thus, pastors and priests should help older adults to deal with their anger issues to prevent the progression of responsive behavior. Hence, older adults who can have anger issues developed by their traumatic experiences can be assisted on how to control their emotions through prayers.

### Prayer Amidst Anger

*Heavenly Father, I bless for your living word, which directs and prepares us for the Great Day when Jesus Christ will come for His bride. Your servant Apostle Paul advised us in Ephesians 4:26 that if I become angry, I should not allow my anger to lead me into sin. It is my desire to obey and please you all days of my life. I pray to walk with you as Moses did, and he died at a prime age, still strong and healthy (Deuteronomy 34:7). My anger can make me sin and separate me from you. I beseech you, Lord, to help my anger, give me sufficient grace to take control of my emotions and put the right words in my mouth to glorify you in all my actions, in the name of Jesus Christ, Amen.*

### Ensuring Safety and Achieving Security

A pastor must understand that the nature of his relationship with the counselee is of the utmost importance to aid traumatized people. It is mostly an issue of ensuring safety (holding environment). The professional code of confidence provides protection, no doubt, but it is insufficient by itself. Additionally, safety within the connection must become clear. For instance, a pastor should never confront terrible incidents on their own. On the other hand, curiosity (the hunt for sensation) is destructive and will lead to an unsafe environment, whereas a concerned interest from a serving and listening attitude is healthy. Before they dare to confront their own experiences, traumatized persons require extra safety. It's not a given that they will ever get to the point where they can talk about those experiences.

Safety promotes confidence and trust between the counselor and counselee. The counselor must ensure there is a safe environment for the counselee in order to make sure the counseling process is effective. Helping the older adults receiving counseling to feel secure is significant in the process of making sure the consequences of their traumatic experiences are effectively managed. When a safe environment is created, the counselee can open up and make it easy to address their issues. The counselor can begin by reading several verses to the counselee about being safe by trusting the Almighty God.

Some of the Bible verses are: Psalm 121:7-8: " The Lord will keep you from all harm- he will watch over your life; the Lord will watch over your coming and going both now and forevermore" (NIV); Psalm 46:1: "God is our refuge and strength, an ever-present help in trouble" (NIV); and 2 Thessalonians 3:3: "But the Lord is faithful, and he will strengthen you and protect you from the evil one" (NIV). These are verses to help the older adults fearful because of the traumatic experiences overcome their fears and feel safe to communicate about their experiences.

A feeling of security should also be mirrored in safety. Literally, "trauma" implies "severe injury." As a result, the wound must be treated with the utmost care while keeping in mind how serious the injury is. Unfortunately, those who have experienced trauma frequently discover that their wounds are exacerbated by insensitive and ignorant responses to their suffering. Having a sense of security makes it simpler to articulate conflicted emotions and enables the counselee to ask God the most incisive whys.

Traumatic experiences have a considerable potential of developing a sense of insecurity among older adults, contributing to a loss of meaning in life. Thus, helping this population to have a sense of security is significant to enable them to have a meaningful life, and improve their emotional and physical health.

*Prayer for Safety and Security*

*O Everlasting God, I honor and glorify your name. It is written that the righteous run to your name and are safe because your name, O God, is a strong tower. We find our joy, meaning in life, and security in your presence. When I read the incident when Jesus Christ, you were with the disciples crossing the Sea of Galilee, and a furious storm came up. I gain courage and feel secure in your presence. While the strong waves were threatening to break the boat, Jesus, you were sound asleep. Lord Jesus, I pray to stay and walk with me because I will be insecure without you. Shield and carry me in your eternal arms, for you are the good shepherd. In your mighty name, I pray. Amen.*

*Facing Traumatic Events*

People will always experience trials, trauma, and tribulations because this is part of life. These three things have a significant impact on how people perceive the world as well as how they relate to other people. Thus, it is imperative for pastors to guide people, especially older adults, to discover what Bible says about trauma, meditate on Bible verses concerning trauma, seek Holy Spirit's guidance in replacing anxiety and fear with truth, and, when possible, join the Biblical community.[11]

---

[11] For an excellent resource on helping in counseling among those who have been traumatized. MacDonald et al.'s *Christ-Centered Biblical Counseling.*

Fig. 5.
A Couple Looking at the Ruins of Their House Destroyed by Fire.

When we read the story of Sarah and Hagar in the book of Genesis, we find how people can experience emotional trauma. Sarah was in her prime age and had no children; this compelled her to devise a strategy to get Abraham, an heir. Hagar, the handmaid, bore Abraham a son Ishmael, but this brought in a traumatic crisis, especially between Sarah and Hagar (Genesis 16:4-5), which caused the handmaid to be sent away with her toddler. However, God went with them and helped Hagar and Ishmael to settle in the wilderness of Paran (Genesis 21:20).

Thus, pastors and priests need to encourage older adults, when counseling them on dealing with traumatic crises, to consider referring to the Bible to draw inspiration, knowledge, and wisdom to navigate difficult situations. God is the one who sees and cares for us (Genesis 16:14; 1 Peter 5:7) and the sheer number of traumatic situations that are described in the Bible means that the Scriptures provide much guidance on how faith can mitigate disaster.

*Prayer for Helping Counselees to Cope with Traumatic Events*

*Many are the tribulations we face through life, O God, and we pray to be able, as You can, to help others endure and grow from tragedy. From the Scriptures we learn of so many who suffered but with your comforting, survived and even thrived. Teach those of us who counsel to be sensitive and skillful in offering comfort and helping others to find meaning even in the face of awesome disaster.*

*Maintaining One's Autonomy*

In addition to protection and security, it's important to offer the client enough room so that autonomy can develop. By autonomy, I don't imply independence from God but rather the ability to once again take charge of one's own life and make independent judgments. It takes a lot of work to encourage and challenge autonomy in traumatized individuals since they frequently feel helpless and powerless. After all, it is typical of traumatic occurrences that the individual who experienced it had no control over the circumstance or very little influence. Because of the trauma, the safe environment was violated, and the individual engaged was out of control. As a result, confidence in God as well as trust in oneself and others can both suffer significant damage.

Clinton and Ohlschlager show that autonomy helps in empowering older adults in order to develop or have control over their life situations and mental health care by instilling personal dignity, respect and value. Also, autonomy plays a significant role in increasing confidence and self-esteem. Additionally, autonomy offers older adults the ability to choose. God created man and gave him the ability to reason and make decisions (free will). Thus, Christian counselors should learn this from God and allow older adults to be able to feel independent but not independent from God. This independence is making their choices and being informed. For instance, trauma-informed care is an intervention that gives an individual autonomy and control in their process of recovery from a traumatic experience.

*Prayer for Autonomy*

*Dear Heavenly Father, I thank you for how you created me. You gave me the ability to know and choose. In the Garden of Eden, Adam and Eve had the ability to decide whether to eat or not to eat the forbidden fruit. This shows me that even though you have ultimate control of your lives, we do have some degree of control over our lives. I beseech you, Lord, to guide me through the helper you gave us, the Holy Spirit, to utilize wisely this ability you have given me. Let your grace be sufficient to me, as I abide by you as the True vine; I will be a productive branch and do everything to honor you. In this situation, as you help me to endure and overcome it, enable me to play my role for your glory God, in Jesus' name. Amen.*

### Helping to Deal with Physical Pain

Integrating the memories and learning to manage them are crucial steps in the trauma-coping process. This is made possible if the client begins to connect with his memories, the discomfort and the worry that occasionally caused unbearable misery. The pastor can help in drawing this link without taking on the suffering himself! (Only Jesus Christ, the Great Pastor, is able to achieve that. He connects people in a way that no one else can, and he doesn't run from any kind of pain.) Traumatic experiences lead to emotional pain that contributes to sadness and anger. Therefore, connecting older adults with their pain is an effective way of managing their pain due to experiencing traumatic crises.

Connecting with pain is a way of accepting the current situation. It is fearful of facing pain or hard times, but embracing the current situations helps in overcoming the intensity of the pain. Apostle Paul speaks about a thorn in his flesh that he prayed thrice to God to take away. However, God did not take it away. Instead, He gave Paul enough grace to endure the pain of the thorn in his flesh. Similarly, when Jesus Christ was to be crucified, he said His spirit was willing to take the cup before Him, but his flesh was refusing. But he decides to yield to the will of his Father. Thus, this activity can be encouraged among older adults with traumatic experiences in order to overcome the pain associated with those events.

### Prayer to Connect with Pain

*Lord Jesus, I honor and adore you. You left the heavenly throne and came to the earth to take the human form in order to feel like I feel right now. You know how it feels to be in physical pain, emotional pain, hungry, deserted and tempted. Therefore, I will not be discouraged by this pain and trauma; I know you will revive and refresh me. After Job went through difficult times to the point of being severely sought, God healed him and restored everything he had lost. My trust and hope are in you, Jehovah-Rapha. You are God who heals, and I believe you will heal me emotionally, physically, and spiritually, in Jesus' name. Amen.*

### Loss of Faith

All too often, as people grow old and face more and more loss of both their friends and the person they used to be, slipping into loss of faith and disbelief happens. When counseling older adults, pastors tend to integrate talk therapy methodologies with theological concepts (Christian belief practices). Mainly, the counselors focus on the navigation of spiritual concerns and day-to-day life struggles experienced by Christians. There is a significant connection between health and spirituality. Thus, Christian counselors should always acknowledge the significance of the spiritual concept in providing care and guidance to older adults with traumatic experiences. Spirituality is epitomized by faith, a search for purpose and meaning in life, a transcendence of self, and a sense of connection with people around, leading to well-being and inner peace.[12] Thus, the strong spiritual connection has considerable potential to improve an individual's satisfaction with life or allow accommodation of a disability.

---

[12] See Delgado's discussion of the concept of spirituality.

Thus, it is important to monitor how the target population believe in the working of God. Faith is crucial among believers, and to be healed, you need to have faith in God. When the woman who had experienced bleeding for 12 years touched, the hem of Jesus' garment was healed. When Jesus turned said your faith has made you whole (Luke 8:40-48). Also, Bartimaeus – the blind man. Received sight because he had faith in Jesus Christ. In Mark 10:52, Jesus says: "Go … your faith has made you well" (RVS). This is a practice that I am addressing under this activity. The counseling process to be effective and helpful to older adults experiencing traumatic events, this spiritual concept should be keenly considered. It does not matter the level of faith they have but must have, even if it is the size of a mustard seed.

### Prayer Facing Unbelief

*Merciful God, I sometimes waiver in my belief that you see and hear me. I wonder if you will answer prayers. I believe, yet I ask you to help my unbelief. Strengthen my belief in You that I may be able to do everything I am called to do. In Jesus' name, I pray, Amen.*

### Coping with Family Issues—Interventions

Some older adults are traumatized by the interactions within their families. When counselors try to engage in the counseling process, it implies the significance of addressing family problems that can prevent the family's healthy functioning. Unhealthy functioning of the family could cause the older adults because that is not what they laid a foundation for or expected. Therefore, it is important to practice engaging parents and children when dealing with older adults with traumatic experiences. Family is the safe haven for man while alive and should be made secure, firm and functioning at all costs.

### Prayer on Family Interventions

*Dear God, I honor you for the family you have given us. I thank you because you value families, and you started the first family in the Garden of Eden. I pray when our family struggles with confusion and fear that, you will grant us the required strength and power to maintain and sustain our family. Unite our family, and fill us with love. Administer to every member of our family, meet their heart desires and help exist to glorify you, our Father. Please help us to overcome our fears and anxieties. In Jesus' name, Amen.*

### *Dealing with Social Isolation*

Social isolation has a real impact on one's emotional and physical health, especially as one ages. The effects of loneliness may be particularly likely to affect people over 60. As a result of the epidemic, older persons are becoming more socially isolated, which may have further negative effects on their health and well-being. Social isolation serves as a useful tool in the battle against the trauma crisis. This has been the most effective way to safeguard yourself from problems that may arise as you age. Therefore, this theory uses two different approaches. First, use social distance to identify the situational context of the aged. Second, to comprehend how they are handling it and coping with themselves in these lonely circumstances. It is considered that once the key elements are known, effective policies can be created for them to protect them during times of crisis.

Proverbs 18:1 says, "A man who isolates himself seeks his own desires; he rages against all wise judgment." It translates to this: Every arrogant recluse must come to his senses, find a human company, and learn to hear counsel. Being alone is bad for both men and women. There is no typical chance of salvation outside of His Church Visible, which is where all followers of Christ belong.

The elderly, in particular, confront significant challenges in their day-to-day lives, just like many others. Don'L undertook a qualitative study of older people to discover the effects of traumatic crisis-related social isolation on their daily lives and current circumstances The primary themes Don'L found were that social relationships are in "theory" as they bind close family ties and distance relationships with their significant others. Figure 10 shows the connections among loneliness, self-talk, feeling, and doing.

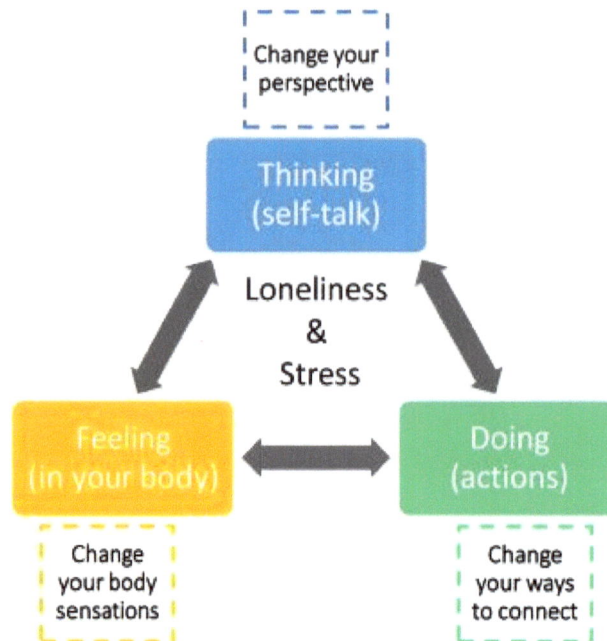

Fig. 11. Actions in Relation to the Experience of Loneliness and Stress

Don'L also documents coping mechanisms used by participants to manage their severe psychological stress. Additionally, it can be beneficial if they are ready to handle their terrible crises. To make their coping mechanisms more effective in dealing with this unanticipated crisis, pastors might design plans and policies based on local or remote area approaches for awareness, counseling, and volunteer activities. Matthew 11:28-29 stated: "Come to me, all you who are weary and burdened, and I will give you rest. Take my yoke upon you and learn from me, for I am gentle and humble in heart, and you will find rest for your souls." There are times when we need to rest and re-group.

*Doing Forgiveness*

Some older adults suffer from trauma because of being hurt by someone. They are traumatized because they are bewildered either to forgive or not to forgive. Unforgiveness can contribute to negative emotions and hinder the healing process. Accepting trauma allows the affected person to take action to make peace with whatever happened. But some people bury a range of emotions under the cover of moving on. However, negative emotions always recur because of a lack of forgiveness. Thus, forgiveness could enable older adults to heal from traumatic experiences.

Counselors should try to understand the causes of the trauma, and when those factors are identified, appropriate action should be taken. Pastors should take their counselees through the Bible to show them how Stephen was stoned but still forgave those who did that before dying. Also, to learn from Jesus Christ, who was brutalized and crucified but forgave those who did that before dying. Thus, forgiveness is a significant component of achieving relational, mental, spiritual, and physical well-being. It involves forgiving yourself and others, thus, creating room for positive thoughts. It is not easy to practice this, but we should ask God to teach and help us.

*Prayer to Be Forgiving and Forgiven*

*Dear God, thank you for your word, which teaches us to forgive because we will be forgiven. I have a heavy heart, and I come to you to help me with this burden. Help to learn how to forgive and let it go. Some people have wronged me, but Father, help me to forgive them. Jesus, you have set an example for us to emulate, help me to walk in your path, O, Lord. Forgive me for not forgiving others as you require me to do. In the name of Jesus Christ, Amen*

**2. Theoretical Bases of Counselling**

The subsections of this part of the Handbook all concern some of the most useful theoretical bases for counselling the elderly. Many of them will be familiar to the reader as ideas that have received broader attention in secular therapy.

*Practicing Emotional Intelligence*

Emotional intelligence (EQ) is regarded as the ability to "identify, understand, and manage" your own and others' emotions (Mullen et al. 113). It is a relatively recent formal concept yet has been implicit in human and divine behavior for thousands of years. EQ is considered to be an important attribute for Christian counselors. EQ involves self-awareness, which is being aware of your weaknesses, strengths, needs, wants, and tendencies. Also, EQ involves empathy and understanding other people's perspectives and emotions. Additionally, EQ is made of relationship management, which relies on effective communication, conflict resolution, and healthy boundaries. Thus, pastoral counselors need to effectively understand the emotions of older adults with traumatic experiences and respond to them appropriately. Research shows pastoral counselors who have poor EQ experience challenges in communicating effectively, managing their emotional responses, and helping counselees to navigate difficult feelings.

Pastoral counselors should always practice EQ to have helpful counseling sessions for elderly people with traumatic crises. Pastors can try to practice hypothetical counselee interactions before their sessions by imagining contingent reactions and how there can appropriately respond. Also, they can consider identifying what might trigger certain emotions and how to respond to them. Also, pastors are required to learn and understand nonverbal communication, including posture and facial expressions.

Jesus teaches about emotional intelligence through the example of His own traits such as the ability to elicit healing trust in sick persons, self-awareness, abundance mentality, optimism, empathy, and stress resilience.[13] Several Bible also call on us to recognize and practice emotional intelligence. For example, Proverbs 17:27 states, "He that hath knowledge spareth his words and a man of understanding is of excellent spirit" (KJV). And, of course, the often-called "Golden Rule" from the sermon on the mount is all about having the emotional intelligence to infer what others need from one's own requirements: from Mathew 7:12, "All things therefore whatsoever ye would that men should do unto you, even so do ye also unto them: for this is the law and the prophets" (ASV). And Proverbs 18:2 warns, "A fool has no delight in understanding" (KJV). In contrast, the counsellor (and the counselee that learns from the scripture), must come to delight in the quiet understanding that goes with EQ, so that, "The words of a man's mouth [become] as deep waters" (Proverbs18:4).

*Prayer for Emotional Intelligence*

*Lead me O Lord, to follow Jesus's way of patient quiet, listening, and understanding of my own and others' feeling. Let me learn to learn what they need to heal and be uplifted. And grant me the ability to recognize my own feelings and needs so that I may act righteously with others. Amen.*

### Expanding One's Horizon: The Hermeneutic View

Hans Georg Gadamer is credited with originally introducing the hermeneutic science idea known as the "horizon of understanding." In the process of understanding, each person carries their own background with them. Our horizon broadens if we allow ourselves to be open to new experiences or learning. The broader the horizon, the better our chances are of learning more. A successful encounter between multiple individuals might be defined as one in which their horizons have fused in some way. Each individual maintains, so to speak, their unique personality and range of experience. As the various horizons come into contact, they

---

[13] For illuminating discussion of the emotional intelligence of Jesus, see Oswald and Jacobson's *The Emotional Intelligence of Jesus: Relational Smarts for Religious Leaders*.

begin to spread out (Fig. 5).

Fig. 6. Turning the Hermeneutical Circle into a Spiral

Biblical hermeneutics is referred to as the branch of knowledge that involves dealing with the interpretation of Biblical verses. This involves looking into the context of the verses and the language used. It is important that pastors practice interpreting There are several Bible passages that relate to reconfiguring one's perspective, making it broader so that older adults understand others and reality (worldly and divine). For instance, Romans 12:2 states. "And be not conformed

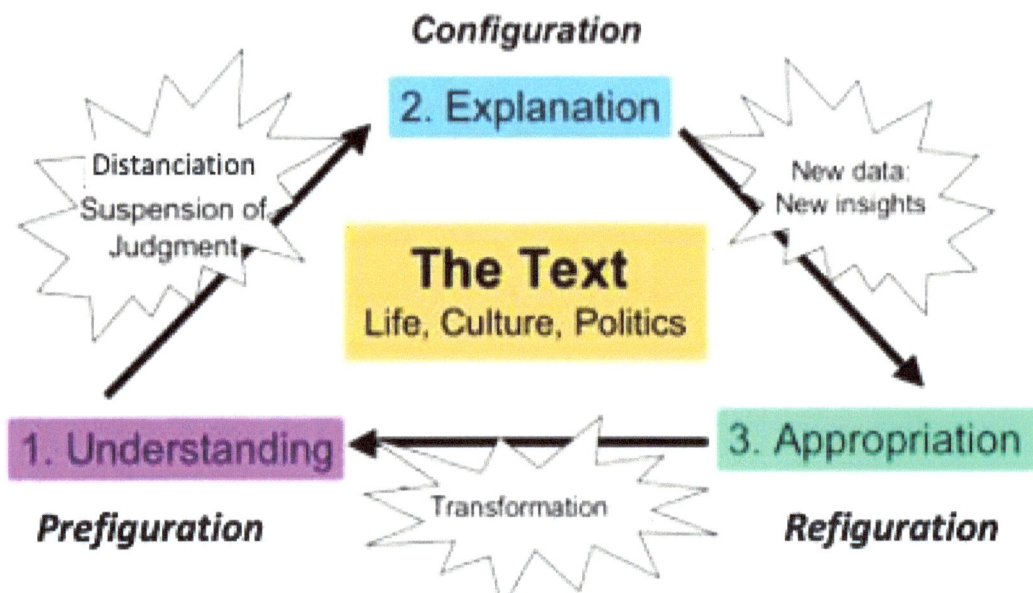

to this world; but be ye transformed by the renewing of your mind" (KJV). And in 2 Corinthians 4:18 the guidance is, "While we look not at the things which seen, but at the things which are not seen; for the things that are seen are temporal; but the things which are not seen are eternal" (KJV).

The book of Job is a good example that pastors can use to interpret to older adults experiencing traumatic crises and how, as Job did, he needed to transform his view of the dire situation and his relationship with God. This approach aims at deepening the understanding of the Bible and how we can relate this understanding to what we face in daily life. Therefore, this activity involves picking a Bible verse, passage or book and interpreting it for the client. The knowledge generated by the interpretation will help in understanding their experiences, and they can face them by relying on the Word of God.

*Prayer for a New Way of Seeing Things*

*Lord, help me to change the way I look at the hardships I encounter in this world. Let me learn from your Word about those who changed the way they looked upon adversity so that they could adapt to the different realities faced in aging. Help me to see the world anew and, in that, know its bounty that you have given humanity.*

### *Applying Theories of Human Trauma*

This era has seen a very large upturn in taking trauma as a common and most serious peril for well-being for all people but notably in the case of the elderly. Christian counselors can consider theories of human trauma on how to deal with the behavior of older adults with traumatic experiences. In this activity, we focus on the theory by Sigmund Freud that suggests human behavior is significantly influenced by unconscious thoughts, memories, and urges. The Freudian theory proposes that the psyche comprises several aspects, such as the ego, superego, and id. The significance of Christian counselors in understanding Freudian theory is because of its influence on contemporary psychologists. The significant contribution of Freud to the psychology of counseling is talk therapy. Talk therapy suggests that when people talk about their problems, it helps in alleviating them.[14]

---

[14] For discussion of talk therapy see Levers.

| Therapist | Client | Outcomes |
|---|---|---|
| Social Engagement → | Neuroception (Safety) → | Improvements in state regulation, social behavior communication skills, quality of life |
| Melodies → | Engage and Exercise Social Engagement System → | |

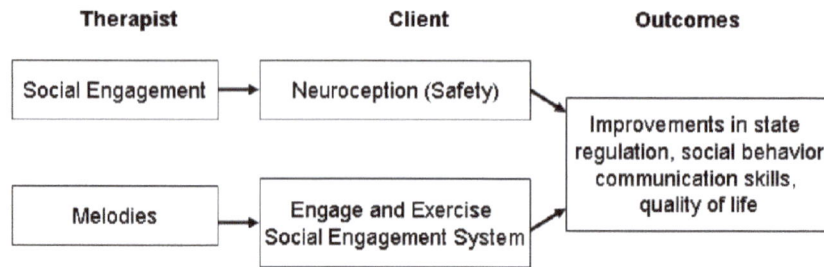

Fig. 7. Diagram of Therapist/Client Process

Miller agrees that everyone who goes through traumatic crises struggles with difficulty and concerns regarding memories of those traumatic events. Thus, a better understanding of the impact of memories will allow Biblical counselors to consider biblical teaching concerning memories to help individuals struggling with traumatic crises, especially the identified population. Therefore, pastors can use this approach when dealing with older adults with traumatic experiences to help them find relief from such events. This allows the counselors to identify issues and find solutions verbally. Also, the talking sessions with the counselors will enable the individuals to forge a path forward through the disorders that have affected their daily activities. Thus, in this way, it is possible for counselors to help their clients to have face life's inevitable trauma: "He shall cover you with His feathers, and under His wings, you shall take refuge; His truth shall be your shield and buckler. You shall not be afraid of the terror by night, nor the arrow that flies by day, nor the pestilence that walk in the darkness, nor the destruction that lays waste at noonday."—Psalm 91:4-6 (WEB)

*Prayer for Those Going Through Traumatic Experiences*

*Gracious God, please grant me the perspective to know that hardship lies in everyone's path and that beyond the hurt, it will make me wiser and more accepting of the fullness of life. Loose me, O God, from the negativity of such experiences and let this trauma teach me and others.*

*Exposure Therapy*

Clinton and Hawkins explain exposure therapy as a clinical intervention involving procedures that contribute to making up a wider cognitive-behavioral approach used in counseling. Exposure therapy is defined as "deliberately confronting some ordinarily avoided stimulus that provokes an undesired response, in order to reduce the strength of that response" (Brady and Raines 51). Hughes notes "Christian clients are a bit surprised when I ask them to practice exposure. Repeating scary, terrible thoughts on paper or aloud. Doing things that feel risky" (para. 1). We can find reference in the Bible to the need sometimes to But he continues with the rationale that "part of the being the church of Christ is to speak the truth including difficult things like anger" (para. 2). We can find support in having to take risks—as needed in exposure therapy— in Corinthians 4:6— "Be careful for nothing, but in every thing by prayer and supplication with thanksgiving let your requests be made known unto God."

Exposure therapy helps in treating fear disorders because it targets avoided stimuli, such as images, people, objects or situations, with an objective of modifying maladaptive behaviors and fears memories by "habituation to cues that elicit the fear response" (Maschi et al. 113). Clinton and Hawkins show that exposure therapy is effective in treating anxiety disorders because it can involve exposure that is prolonged or repeated, as well as in vivo or imaginal. When the right procedures are followed, exposure therapy is effective in addressing; panic disorder, post-traumatic stress disorder (PTSD), obsessive-compulsive disorder (OCD), generalized anxiety disorder (GAD), and phobias among older adults. Additionally, studies show this intervention has been useful in managing chronic pain, depression, and difficult bereavement.

When pastors and priests decide to use this intervention to counsel older adults with traumatic experiences, they will have to gradually habituate their clients to heightened arousal in response to avoided stimuli. Thus, the counselees actively participate in the activity in order to "clarify the arousal-avoidance response cycle; to develop the graded hierarchy of arousal and anxiety; to actively practice relaxation and other adaptive strategies; to direct the type, timing, and amount of exposure; to process in-session thoughts and feelings related to exposure; and to practice exposure therapy outside of formal counseling sessions." (Brady and Raines 122).

*Prayer for Success in Using Exposure Therapy*

*Dear Lord, grant me the courage to explore the unknown and the difficult as a way to learning about myself that leads to peace and righteousness. Teach me with the examples from the Holy Scriptures of how your people took chances in matters small and large and so learned to overcome their fear. Amen.*

*Using Talk Therapy*

Proverbs 15:22: "Without counsel, purposes are disappointed: but in the multitute of counsellors they are established" (KJV).

Talk therapy really means any form of counselling that centers on the client speaking feely about her or his life and problems—As discussed earlier, person-centered therapy is especially focused on encouraging the counselee to take a lead in discussion. When Christian counselors practice talk therapy, they help older adults by gaining an understanding of their emotions, overcoming anxiety and insecurities, coping with stress, identifying roadblocks to optimal mental health, and processing previous traumatic experiences. God encourages us to disclose our problems to one another. Thus, talk therapy is effective in helping older adults with traumatic experiences. In James 5:16, the Word of God says, "Therefore confess your sins to each other and pray for each other so that you may be healed. The prayer of a righteous person is powerful and effective" (NIV). Also, Galatians 6:2 encourages us: "Bear ye one another's burdens, and so fulfil the law of Christ" (KJV)—and this can be achieved through talking and opening up to others.

***Prayer for the Counselee to Open Up in Discussions***

*Dear Lord, we know that in the end wisdom comes from your guidance, but we ask that those who are being counseled find their voice to tell counsellors what has been going on, what they eventually want to change. Help them to speak their truths and lives and help those who they turn to, to hear and find the wisdom in what they know about their lives.*

### Adlerian Theory: Encouragement

Alfred Adler was a colleague of Simon Freud but who diverged Freud in developing psychotherapy that "envisioned a psychology of growth, where people could strive to overcome difficulties and actually change their lives" (Carson and Engler-Carson 3). Based on Adlerian theory, encouragement is one of the key concepts. This concept emphasizes the dignity and worth of every human being and expresses an optimistic outlook confirming that individuals can decide, create, and act for positive change. Encouragement is considered to be crucial for human development and growth. This is shown to be effective regarding talk therapy (psychotherapy) Figure 8 is a process diagram showing the onset of psychological dysfunction and the use of an Adlerian approach to dealing with such condictiones.

Adler emphasized the significance of encouragement when he made a statement in 1956, "Altogether, in every step of the treatment, we must not deviate from the path of encouragement" (Adler 342). Encouragement refers to a way of relating to others, which covers both relationship-building and attitudinal skills.

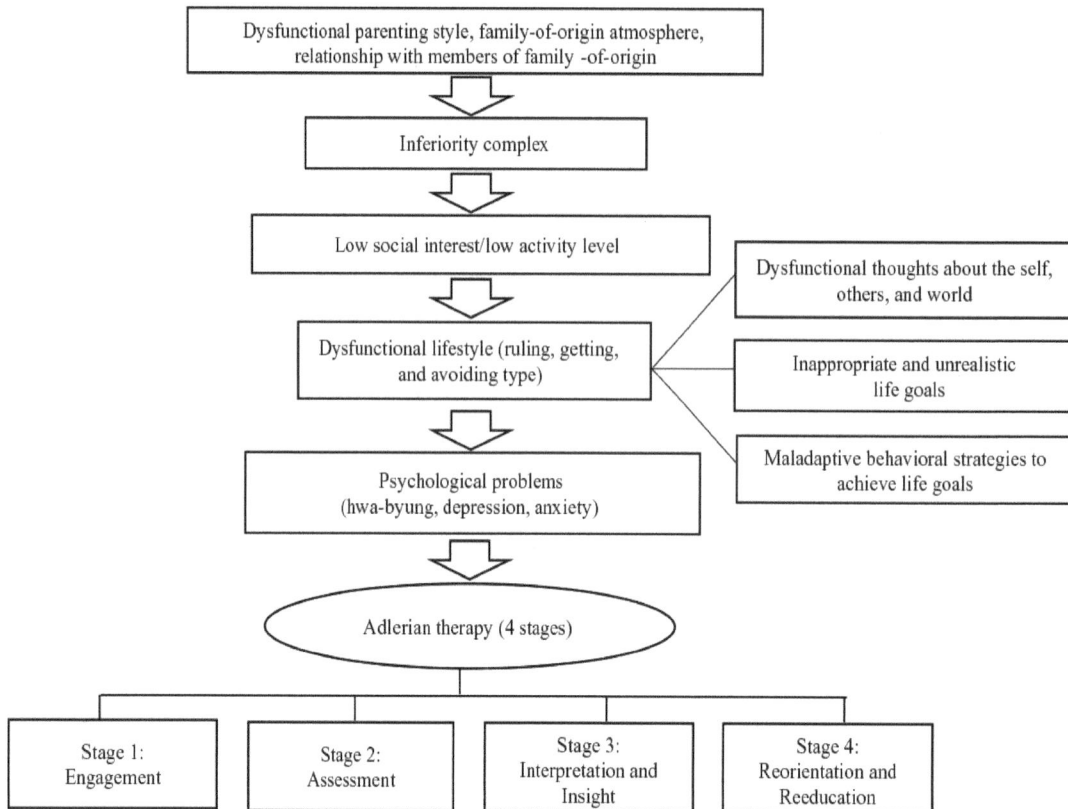

Fig.9. Elements of Applying Adlerian Therapy to Counseling and Healing

Encouragement contributes to positive psychology, which involves shifting from pathology to wellness. Before I addressed how traumatic experiences contribute to negative attitudes and thinking. However, when pastors consider encouragement in counseling through the Bible, older adults' well-being is improved. Also, encouragement promotes optimism which helps in fighting against depression and enhances resilience. This shows that older adults develop their strength when they are encouraged to face their hard times with a positive mindset. 1 Peter 1:6-7 says, "So be truly glad. There is wonderful joy ahead, even though you must endure many trials for a little while. These trials will show that your faith is genuine. It is being tested as fire tests and purifies gold" (NLT). God allows life challenges to make us strong; thus, when older adults are encouraged with Bible verses like 1 Peter 1:6-7, they are highly motivated to move on with life with more hope

of better things.

*Prayer of Thanks for Faith and Its Continuing*

*Dear Lord Jesus, I thank you because you know the experiences of this world since you came into the world as one of us. You went through significant suffering to the point of death. As I face trials in my life, I pray to strengthen and help me always remember that you are always with me in all circumstances and. Make your grace sufficient to me that I will keep the faith because great joy awaits me. In the name of Jesus Christ, I pray, Amen.*

### *Solution-Focused Brief Therapy*

Clinton and Ohlschlager describe solution-focused brief therapy (SFBT) as goal-oriented,

future-focused, and pays attention to solutions rather than the issues or problems that led the client

to seek counseling. Figure 11 is a commonly used diagram of the interlocking pieces of SFBT.

Fig. 12. Elements of Solution-Focused Brief Therapy. From Preet Sandhu, *What is Solution-Based Brief Therapy?* Fresh Perspective Counseling.
https://www.fpcounseling.com/blog/what-is-solution-focused-brief-therapy

SFBT is an evidence-based therapeutic intervention that integrates positive psychology practices and principles to help counselees change by developing solutions. SBFT is considered a friendly, future-oriented, positive electing vehicle for motivating, formulating, sustaining, and achieving the desired change. This form of therapy is useful in Christian counseling because it focuses on the counselees' present moment and future needs. It tries to develop clients' skills based on their current strengths that can enable them to move forward with life. The main purpose of counseling older adults with traumatic experiences is to help them move on with life rather than focusing on what happened to them.

Isaiah 43:18 says, "Do not remember the former things, Nor consider the things of old. Behold, I will do a new thing" (NKJV). God admonishes us not to focus on past experiences and requires us to hope for better things from the present to the future. This is the core of this therapy. It goes hand in hand with living in the present and also, not becoming obsessed with what may later happen, any more than what already has. Matthew 6:34 from the closing of the Sermon on the Mount, states, "Take therefore no thought for the morrow: for the morrow shall take thought for the things of itself. Sufficient unto the day is the evil thereof" (KJV).

Thus, this therapy will help older adults with traumatic crises to look for the positive side of the situations they are going through with the hope of better tomorrow. SFBT will strengthen the counselees to cope with their current hardships looking for a better future. This is a therapy that encourages optimism – and hope keeps us alive. Hope develops endurance and patience, which are encouraged in the Christian life.

### Prayer for Living in the Present

*My Lord, help me to see that the past is over, the future not yet come and that the righteous living that I aspire to, must be practiced in the here and now. Help to lose obsession about "should have beens" and, likewise of the unknowable future. And let me see what needs to be done now to align my life with your teachings. Amen.*

*Using Operant Conditioning for Counselee Adaptability*

Behavioral modification involves a regular schedule of rewards and punishments in order to change or learn behavior. Operant conditioning involves learning used in behavioral psychology that emphasizes the impact of rewards and punishments on specific behaviors. The objective of this theory is to reinforce acceptable behaviors by giving rewards and eliminate unwanted behaviors by using targeted punishments. Behavioral therapies are more action-based and use learned strategies to prevent developing undesirable behaviors. Traumatic events lead to unwanted behaviors such as emotional upset, anxiety, or depressive symptoms, difficulties with self-regulation, relationship issues, regression, etc. Thus, operant conditioning will play a significant role in regulating the development of these undesirable behaviors.

God uses the system of rewards and punishments to promote good practices and discourage bad behaviors. 2 Chronicles 7:14 says, "if My people, who are called by My name, shall humble themselves and pray, and seek My face and turn from their wicked ways, then will I hear from heaven, and will forgive their sin and will heal their land" (KJ). This verse shows us God rewards those who do according to what He requires. When people do not do what God requires are punished. Zachariah 14:7 says, "If any of the peoples of the earth do not go up to Jerusalem to worship the King, the LORD Almighty, they will have no rain" (NIV).

*Prayer for Adaptability*

*Dear God, I honor you for preserving and sustaining me. I thank you because your word tells us in the book of James 1:2 that we should consider troubles that come our way as an opportunity for great joy. I am going through tough times that have the potential to make me develop negative attitudes about my life. How I pray, dear Father, to enable me to live according to your will! Free me from the shackles of a negative attitude. Working to transform my thinking pattern from negative to positive for your glory Lord, regardless of my struggles. Give me joy that comes from you. In Jesus' name, Amen.*

*Moving Towards Mindfulness*

In the past several decades, the long history of meditation and solitude has become an actual technique that is widely discussed and practiced—*mindfulness*. It is often defined as holding one's mind fully in the present and not letting it wander off into past difficulties or future events. Research shows a relationship between trauma and mindfulness meditation. Both aspects are embedded in sensory experience. Trauma contributes to stress, but mindfulness plays a significant role in reducing stress. Studies show that everyone who has experienced trauma can benefit from

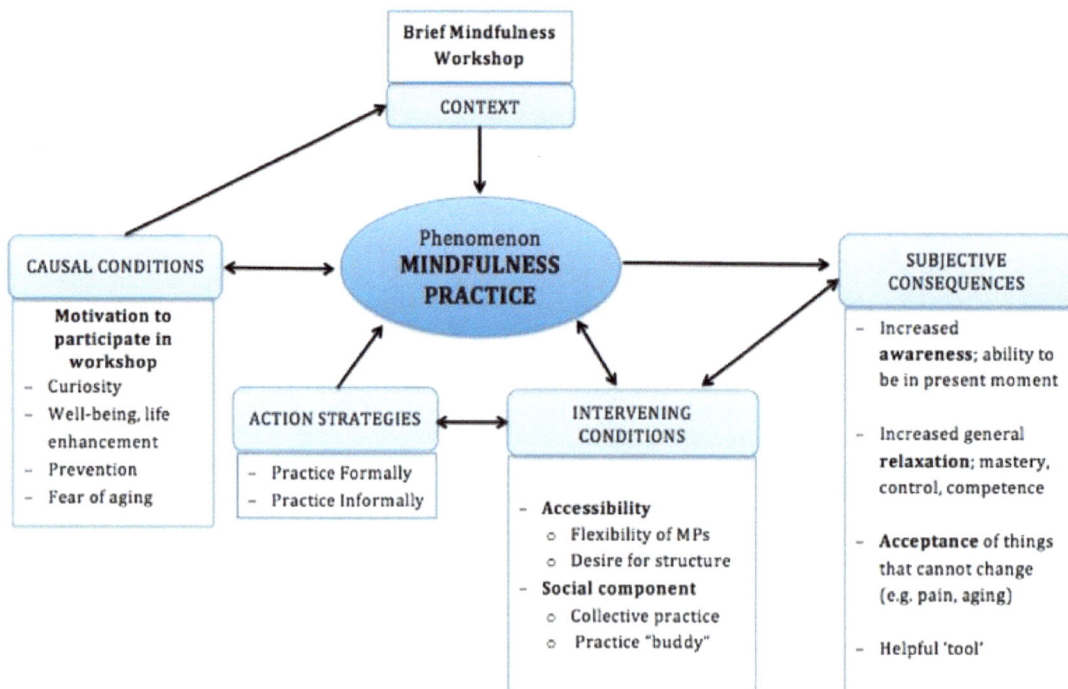

meditation. Figure 9 outlines key elements of mindfulness practice.

Fig. 10.  Key Elements of Mindfulness Practice

Mindfulness meditation is useful in bringing to an end the exacerbating symptoms of stress associated with traumatic experiences. Practicing mindfulness is significant among older adults with traumatic experiences because it improves present-moment awareness, strengthens the personal ability for self-regulation, and increases self-compassion. These are important skills that are useful in trauma recovery.

Mindfulness meditation should be encouraged in line with the word of God. God told Joshua, "This Book of the Law must not depart from your mouth; meditate on it day and night, so that you may be careful to do everything written in it. For then you will prosper and succeed in all you do" (Joshua 1:8, BSB). Mindfulness meditation should be anchored on the Word of God to mediate what God says about the present situation. This practice will help older adults undergoing traumatic events overcome the effects of the events.

*Prayer for Mindfulness*

*Dear God, your word is clear to us that we should meditate on your law both day and night. You require us to keep your Law throughout our lifetime. I thank you because you have said you will write your commands in the template of my heart. Your word has found a place in my heart. Help to meditate on your word at all times; even when I face hardships, grant me your grace that I will always cling to your word. Your word brings healing, motivation and comfort. Always feed me with your word, in Jesus' name, Amen.*

*pray, Amen.*

### 3. Specific Techniques of Intervention

This section moves from broad theoretical perspectives down to the level of a variety of specific techniques that the biblical counsellor needs in her/his toolkit as each new case is taken on. Not all will be useful in every situation but the more experienced a counsellor gets the more they will be able to selectively find techniques for helping the older client.

*Music Therapy: Using Music to Build Faith and Courage*

Danielson and Ray-Degges studied traumatic experiences among older adults and found that music is a powerful tool used to evoke strong emotions, provide a way of expression and bring back memories. Also, the authors found that older adults can benefit from music therapy because it offers an outlet for socialization, creativity, and mental stimulation. Music therapy has been established as an effective treatment plan for elderly people with Alzheimer's disease.[15] The type of musical therapy recommended here for older adults in the Christian community is receptive music therapy. This type of music therapy involves mindful listening to Christian songs regarding courage and faith. They include songs that encourage older adults to persevere through their experiences and affirm their faith in God. Romans 10:17 tells us: "So then, faith comes from hearing the message, and the message comes through preaching Christ" (RSV). Christian songs play the role of preaching the Good News.

Listening and reflecting on Christian songs provides comfort, encouragement, and inspiration to move on with life despite going through hard times. Pastors are recommended to advise older adults with traumatic experiences to listen to songs such as *You Are My Hiding Place* written by Michael Ledner, right out of Psalms, *What A Friend We Have in Jesus*, written by Charles Crozat Converse and Joseph Medlicott Scriven, *Great Is Thy Faithfulness* by Thomas

---

[15] See Mazokopakis for a discussion of music therapy in the Christian tradition.

Chisholm, and *My World Needs You* by Kirk Franklin, Sarah Reeves, Tasha Cobbs and Tamela Mann.

### Using Talk Therapy

Proverbs 15:22 "Without counsel, purposes are disappointed: but in the multitude of counsellors, they are established "(KJV)

Talk therapy really means any form of counselling that centers on the client speaking feely about her or his life and problems—As discussed earlier, person-centered therapy is especially focused on encouraging the counselee to take a lead in discussion. When Christian counselors practice talk therapy, they help older adults by gaining an understanding of their emotions, overcoming anxiety and insecurities, coping with stress, identifying roadblocks to optimal mental health, and processing previous traumatic experiences. God encourages us to disclose our problems to one another. Thus, talk therapy is effective in helping older adults with traumatic experiences. In James 5:16, the Word of God says, "Therefore confess your sins to each other and pray for each other so that you may be healed. The prayer of a righteous person is powerful and effective" (NIV). Also, Galatians 6:2 encourages us: "Bear ye one another's burdens, and so fulfil the law of Christ" (KJV)—and this can be achieved through talking and opening up to others.

### Prayer for the Counselee to Open Up in Discussions

*Dear Lord, we know that in the end wisdom comes from your guidance, but we ask that those who are being counseled find their voice to tell counsellors what has been going on, what they eventually want to change. Help them to speak their truths and lives and help those who they turn to, to hear and find the wisdom in what they know about their lives.*

### Building Resilience

Older adults can frequently accept the challenges of life without losing sight of why they still wish to live. They also frequently recognize the importance of expressing appreciation and forgiveness rather than holding grudges from the past, which can promote good ageing. Even when it's unexpected or unavoidable, adversity can be processed and conquered with the help of resilience (like the pandemic). People who lack resilience may be more likely to engage in unhealthy coping mechanisms like substance misuse because they find it difficult to survive periods of radical change.

Pastors and priests need to make older adults to understand that God allows some situations in our lives to make us stronger. Apostle Paul says the strength of God is made perfect in our weaknesses (2 Corinthians 12:9-11). Thus, encouraging this population on the essence of becoming resilient is imperative and in line with God's will. Older adults should be made not feel like they are being punished when going through these traumatic events but should feel as a way of being made better by God.

***Prayer For Resilience***

*Dear God, thank you for the life you have given me, your protection and guidance. I thank you for what you have brought me this far, and I call you Ebeneezer. Your word has taught me that in valleys and on mountains, you are with me. Psalms 27:5 says: "In the times of trouble, he will shelter me; he will keep me safe in his temple and make me secure on a high rock." In these hard times, I find refuge in you, my Heavenly Father. I feel weak, and things are going in the wrong direction, but my trust is in you, and U know you are concerned with my welfare. I pray to give me strength and resilience like Apostle Paul. Revive my spirit and refresh my soul; let me find calm, hope and wisdom in you, Everlasting One. Thank you for hearing my prayer, for I have asked this in the name of Jesus Christ. Amen.*

***Shifting to Positivity***

Positive thinking is an activity that helps in managing traumatic experiences and improves an individual's health. When older adults go through traumatic experiences are prone to having their self-talk significantly affected. For instance, most older adults with older adults have their self-talk distressingly negative. This contributes to the individual feeling worse, depressed, fearful or angry. Positive thinking plays an important role in reflecting an individual's outlook on life, determines whether a person is pessimistic or optimistic, reflects an attitude about yourself, and it significantly affects a person's health status. Studies show personality traits, including optimism and pessimism, significantly affect various areas of health and well-being.

Thus, positive thinking is essential because it develops optimism, which plays a part in stress management. So, positive thinking is a skill that older adults can be taught in order to approach unpleasant situations in a more productive and positive way. This means this target population is encouraged and made to believe the best is going to happen despite going through hard times. Pastors and priests should show older adults the essence of practicing positive self-talk and thinking because it helps increase confidence, enhance coping skills, lower stress levels, and other benefits.

### Prayer for a Positive Mindset

*Dear Heavenly Father, I bless and honor you because you created me with a purpose. I thank you because you watch over me day and night. There are other battles that you have fought for me, even without my knowledge. All glory and praises belong to you, the One who sees me through hears my cries, and is pleased to load with me with benefits on a daily basis. The thoughts that you have for me are better and are to give me hope and a bright future. I firmly stand on your word in Jeremiah 29:11, which says: "I alone know the plans that I have for you, plans to bring you prosperity and not a disaster, plans to bring about the future you hope for" (RVS). My hope is in you, and I believe you are going to change things for the better because you meet the heart desires of the ones who delight in you, in Jesus' name. Amen.*

### Empathetic Guidance

It is crucial to adopt a mindset of empathic counseling, go on the search with the counselee, and never step beyond the lines set by the other. The information that the counselee chooses to provide must be entirely under their control. When older adults experience a traumatic crisis, they need guidance to navigate the way to recovery. This means the pastors will have to walk with their clients to heal from their traumatic experiences. The counselors should live what they tell the counselees to do or embrace. This will involve sharing their experiences, if they have any, with the older adults experiencing a traumatic crisis to strengthen and encourage them.

Emphatic guidance is an activity that enables older adults with traumatic experiences to feel they have the necessary support to face their life situations. Emphatic guidance creates room for compassion. Being compassionate is doing according to God's will. The most well-known story of empathy from the Scriptures is probably Jesus's parable of the Good Samaritan (Luke 10:23–37) but the Bible also tells us in the book of Ephesians 4:32: "Be kind and compassionate to one another, forgiving each other, just as Christ God forgave you" Also, emphatic guidance is anchored on Romans 12:15, which says, "Rejoice with those who rejoice; mourn with those who mourn." Other Bible verses that pastors and the counselee should explore are Zechariah 7:9-10; 1 Peter 4:10; Colossians 3:12; and Psalm 112:4. These Bible verses will motivate older adults receiving counseling and feel they have enough support as they deal with traumas, and this will ease them to heal from their traumatic experiences.

*Prayer for Empathy*

*Gracious God, you have given us the blessing of living with others whether family, neighbors or those we counsel. Help us to see the world as they see it and from this empathy, which we follow your example, to reach across differences and understand the lives and tribulations of others, and acting in that knowledge to help them as we can.*

## Providing Non-Anxious Presence

Since worries of all kinds play such a significant part, Edwin Friedman's leadership advice is extremely applicable here. He talks about a "non-anxious presence" that refuses to follow fear and stays far away from a random "quick fix" in which something needs to be fixed, eliminated, or "dealt with." Due to this, I choose the phrase "coping with trauma" rather than "dealing with trauma" (as if it can be dealt with). To break down the isolation and diminish the loneliness the goal must be to find a means to connect with the counselee and provide the opportunity to connect with his or her suffering.

A non-anxious presence is regarded as one of the most powerful and uplifting things used by counselors for their clients. The term describes an individual who offers a cool, calm, collected and focused environment that enables others to manage their hard life situations. Enabling clients to attain a non-anxious presence helps Christian counselors to model emotional regulation that exposes other feelings apart from anxiety. This activity is aimed at bringing about calmness and clarity in the midst of traumatic crises.

*Prayer For Non-Anxious Presence*

*O loving and caring God, you are the one who gives us peace and calms our troubled hearts. My life is a turbulent sea. I cannot find peace and balance; I constantly stumble and worry about my life. You are the Prince of Peace according to Isaiah 9:6; grant me peace and clarity of mind that I will navigate this turbulent sea. Order my steps so I will walk on the right path that leads to a peaceful and better life. You ask if the earthly fathers know the best gifts for their children, how much are you willing to give us the best things? I pray to experience your goodness, O faithful God. I bless you and thank you because you keep your promises, and you are not like a man to tell lies or change his mind. In Jesus' name, I pray. Amen.*

### Monitoring and Enhancing Physical Well-Being

Physical exercises are useful to help older adults to health from traumatic experiences. When older adults are exposed to traumatic events, they tend to experience a variety of emotions, including sadness, fear, grief, and anger. These emotions have a profound impact on physical, social, and psychological health. The impacts range from weight fluctuations, increased sedentary behaviors, social isolation, depressed mood, and increased anxiety to poor sleep hygiene.

Fortunately, when exercise is administered appropriately, it helps to address these issues. Physical exercise should be administered with smart goals. CDC (Centers for Disease Control and Prevention) describes physical activity as one thing that promotes healthy ageing.

Older adults struggling with traumatic experiences and aftermath can be counseled to engage in physical activity to improve their well-being. Studies show physical activities delay or prevent many health problems that accompany ageing. Also, it helps muscles to grow stronger, such that older adults will not solely rely on others to do their day-to-day activities. Therefore, when designing the right activities for this population age, the counsellors are a major consideration. Bible supports healthy and godly living. Paul tells Timothy in, "Keep yourself in training for a godly life. Physical exercise has some value, but spiritual exercise is valuable in every way because it promises life both for the present and for the future" (1 Timothy 4:7-8, GNTA). Our body show is taken care of as a way to honor and glorify God and to improve our health.

***Prayer for Physical Health and Fitness***
*We thank thee, Lord, for our physical bodies and for watching over us through life. Help us to be mindful that our bodies are your gift and must be honored in the way that eat, move and exercise—especially as we age. Encourage me to be as fit as I can be recognizing that my mind and spirit are one with the body throughout life. Amen.*

### Monitoring and Managing Emotional Health

Emotional concepts are essential in the context of mental health. Emotion concepts enable people to understand, predict and experience human behavior. Emotional concepts link the abstract realm with the realm of actions and bodily experience. Emotions are more often interchanged with moods and feelings, but the three are distinctively independent. Kövecses defines emotion as "a complex reaction pattern, involving experiential, behavioral and physiological elements" (34). Thus, emotion expresses how individuals address situations or issues they find personally important. Emotional experiences have several components, including a physiological response, a subjective experience, and an expressive or behavioral response.

Traumatic crises contribute to significant emotional experiences. The traumatic events act as a stimulus to the emotional experiences among older adults. When these events stimulate people, they physiologically respond, which determines how they behave. Thus, when counselors consider this activity, it helps older adults deal with the emotions evoked by traumatic events. This will put elderly people in a position to manage their emotional health. When emotional concepts are regularly monitored, it helps to improve how older adults think and feel. Thus, it contributes to enhancing the sense of well-being, the ability to cope with traumatic events, and recognize their emotions.

### Prayer for Emotional Healing

*Loving and Faithful, Lord, I thank you for knowing how I feel right now. I am emotionally unstable and cannot find my way out of this distressed situation. I feel overwhelmed by emotions and have lost control over my life. Please, Heavenly Father, I ask for your deliverance and emotional healing. You promise to deliver those in trouble and downhearted. So, I wait on you, Lord, to save and lead me on the right path. I absolutely rely on you for deliverance and healing. In Jesus' name, Amen.*

### Encouraging Activities that Increase Self Esteem

Activities that increase self-esteem may include making social bonds and having good habits of personal hygiene.

*Making social bonds*. Personal ties that matter help us feel grounded and more confident. According to research, seniors who have the support of their immediate family and friends tend to have better levels of self-esteem than those who live alone. It's a catch-22, too because seniors with low self-esteem may find it challenging to maintain strong friendships as they get older. If this describes you, start out modestly![16]

*Having a good personal hygiene.* No one feels good about themselves if they spend the entire day lounging around in their pajamas, regardless of their age. When you think of yourself as deserving of care, you start to feel good about yourself. If you are retiring and spending more time alone, it is easy to let your personal hygiene slip. Take the time to get out of bed, take a bath, and get dressed as if you were expecting the company to enhance your confidence.

"I can do all things through Christ who strengtheneth me" (Philippians 4:13, KJV). The following prayer is to rid yourself of the things that cause your lack of confidence. Build your confidence by repeating the Bible verse: "Be strong and of good courage; be not afraid…for the Lord, thy God is with you whithersoever thou you goest" (Joshua 1:9, KJV)

*Prayer for Self-Esteem*

*Dear God, show me how to be a faithful steward of my one and only opportunity to magnify the greatness you have placed within me and to show your presence in my life. Lead me away from complacency and any temptation to settle for less than what you know is my absolute best for me. In Jesus' name. Amen.*

### Engaging with One's Community

Engaging the whole Christian community (church members, family, primary care providers, social workers, and other stakeholders) is a significant strategy for helping older adults with traumatic crises. The CDC states that pastoral counseling is appropriate and effective "when everyone in the Christian community knows and feels secure in the knowledge that as valued members of that community, they can participate in giving and receiving encouragement, guidance,

---

[16] This message is well explained by Kohls.

and support" (434). Policies and programs need to be designed to provide opportunities for the community to take part in the decision-making process and contribute to the well-being of the community members. Engaging the community in counseling practice helps in developing and establishing a healthy system to support older adults with traumatic experiences to receive better counseling and mental health services.

The Acts of Apostles provide us with different examples of the essence of community engagement. The early Christians had the habit of regularly meeting together, worshiping together, and eating together. As a result of meeting regularly, Lord Jesus added their number (Acts 2:46). And Hebrews 10:25 encourages us to keep the habit of meeting together. Thus, meeting together has a therapeutic effect on people with challenges in life within the Christian community. Hence, it is imperative for pastoral counselors to consider this activity more often to improve the health and well-being of older adults undergoing traumatic crises within the Christian community. God created us in a way that we depend on each other. This is why Romans 12:15 says, "Rejoice with those who rejoice and weep with those who weep" (NET).

*Prayer for Community Engagement*

*Dear God, thank you for when you created our first parents, you told them to be multiplied in order to fill the earth. Since the beginning, you gave people the ability to live as a community. 1 Thessalonians 5:14-15 tells us to admonish one another, encourage the fainthearted, help the weak, and practice patience with all men. Father, help to love. Care and live in harmony with one another. Help the church to have the mind of Christ to live as you require us to live, in Jesus' name. Amen.*

### *Drawing on Recurring Themes and Missteps*

While the lives of counselees may appear at first blush to be highly complex stories that are difficult to grasp, a key to therapy is seeing patterns, watching for problems that happen again and again. If the client has been learning and changing through this personal history, then that is positive and important. But all too often, instead people seem to ceaselessly repeat what has been troubling in the past. Self-defeating habits and patterns can be especially disheartening, yet are the "raw material" for reflecting on what needs to change and how.

Pastors can identify the recurrence of specific issues related to the factors that have contributed to traumatic crises among older adults. "Just as the worship community is present in spirit in the counseling room, so the counseling situation can be a part of corporate worship experiences if it is handled very carefully" (Krause 76). This implies that pastors should be sensitive when counseling older adults with traumatic experiences to denote the readily emerging themes that indicate human conditions, especially among people in their late life. For instance, pastors can identify that older adults experience traumatic crises because of social isolation as the major factor. Thus, this issue will be determined to be not confined to the older adults seeking counseling but as a factor affecting this target population; thus, it would be easy to come up with strategies to help this population.

God has created the universe so that people can learn from nature, our surroundings. We gain knowledge from our environment and experiences; we apply it in order daily lives to improve the quality of our lives and others. For instance, Proverbs 6:6-8 tells the indolent: "Lazy people should learn a lesson from the way ants live. They have no leader, chief, or ruler, but they store up their food during the summer, getting ready for winter" (GNBUK). Thus, to make their counseling sessions helpful to the Christian community, pastors should be drawing on the repetitive issues to help the people undergoing such problems and prevent others from getting the same lingo of problems.

**Prayer to Learn from Error**
*Dear Lord, my life sometimes seems like an endless repetition of that which has harmed me and others. Help me, O Lord, to begin to see this recurrence, to learn from my error and sins against You and others, and in this way, steadily move into a different path, one of righteous action.*

### *Bringing Out Accomplishments as a Counseling Technique*

Christian counselors should help older adults see their accomplishments in life. This helps them become more positive about life regardless of the traumatic crisis. Jeremiah 29:11 says, "For I know the plans I have for you, declares the Lord, plans for welfare and not for evil, to give you a future and a hope" (NIV). This verse helps people become positive. This helps in having proper mental health.

Philippians 4:6-7 states, "Be anxious for nothing, but in everything by prayer and supplication, with thanksgiving, let your requests be made known to God; and the peace of God, which surpasses all understanding, will guard your hearts and minds through Christ Jesus (ESV).

Perhaps most encouragingly, Jesus said this about having faith not only in God but in one's self: "For verily I say unto you, That whosoever shall say unto this mountain, Be thou removed, and be thou cast into the sea; and shall not doubt in his heart, but shall believe that those things which he saith shall come to pass; he shall have whatsoever he saith." (Mark 11:23)

With such Scriptural guidance, the counselor has a way to probe—or better yet, have the client probe and recall—what they have succeeded in in life with God's help.

### *Prayer for Recognizing One's Accomplishments*

*Father, I thank you for helping me see what I have achieved in life though many are the struggles of the past, present and, I know, in my future. I have fought with self-doubt and pray that you continue to help me overcome this. Let me compassionate to myself as seek to be with others. Above all, let me see myself as you see me, a child and faithful servant in your care, forever. Amen.*

### *Drawing on Recurring Themes*

Pastors can identify the recurrence of specific issues related to the factors that have contributed to crises for older adults. "Just as the worship community is present in spirit in the counseling room, so the counseling situation can be a part of corporate worship experiences if it is handled very carefully" (Krause 76). This implies that pastors should be sensitive when counseling older adults with traumatic experiences to denote the readily emerging themes that indicate human conditions, especially among people in their late life. In the Bible, there are numerous passages that address the self-defeating repetition of ineffective actions. This is sometimes called "repeating folly" as in Proverbs 15:21 which even suggests that some hard-to-fathom enjoyment can be associated with such behavior: "Folly is joy to him who is destitute of discernment" (KJV). Scripturally based counsellors will try to subtly open the client's eyes to such patterns. For example, it may be that they can identify how some older adults experience traumatic crises because they put themselves into harmful situations over and over. Thus, this issue will be determined to be not confined to the older adults seeking counseling but as a factor affecting this target population; thus, it would be easy to come up with strategies to help this population.

God has created the universe so that people can learn from nature, our surroundings. We gain knowledge from our environment and experiences; we apply it in order daily lives to improve the quality of our lives and others. For instance, Proverbs 6:6-8 tells the lazy people, "Lazy people should learn a lesson from the way ants live. They have no leader, chief, or ruler, but they store up their food during the summer, getting ready for winter" (GNBUK). Thus, to make their counseling sessions helpful to the Christian community, pastors should practice drawing on the repetitive issues to help the people undergoing such problems and prevent others from getting the same lingo of problems.

*Prayer for Recognizing and Ending Self-Destructive Behavior*
*Heavenly Father, I acknowledge that in my life I have often repeated behavior that leads to my own and others' suffering. Help me to identify such patterns and to change my habits to acting in different ways that make life better not worse. Amen.*

### House Calls: Visiting and Encouraging Fellowship with Other Older People

Pastoral counselors should organize how the small groups of church members will be visiting older adults with traumatic experiences. This will involve engaging the church in a special way in the counseling process. When those small groups visit, the target population will be prepared with a sermon and spiritual hymns. This activity is another way of providing social and moral support. Some of the older adults with traumatic crises would have challenges going to church meetings; thus, these home fellowships will play a significant role in encouraging them in the journey of faith. Also, this will be in the context of the Bible, where Jesus prayed for Simon Peter's sick mother-in-law. Luke 4:38-39 says, "Jesus left the synagogue and went to the home of Simon. Now Simon's mother-in-law was suffering from a high fever, and they asked Jesus to help her. So he bent over her and rebuked the fever, and it left her. She got up at once and began to wait on them" (NIV). In Proverbs 18:1. The reason for self-isolation is explained, "He that separateth himself seeketh *his own* desire, And rageth against all sound wisdom" (ASV).

When the apostles were in the ministry through Acts of Apostles and the Epistles, home fellowships were identified in different passages. Thus, this practice should be continued in honor of God and to glorify him. Home fellowship is an expression of love and compassion that the Bible requires to have and to show to one another. Therefore, pastoral counselors should consider this activity to make their services effective.

### Prayer About Visiting and Fellowship with Neighbors

*My God, I see that as I have aged, I have steadily withdrawn from interactions with other older neighbors leading to loneliness, my own and theirs. Help me to have the wherewithal to recognize that those are needless losses and that I can once again, take the time to go out in my own neighborhood and renew old friendships and make new ones.*

## 4. Biblically-Based Counselling Techniques

This section is really a subset of the previous one but is more specifically directed at pastoral care. It rightly places special emphasis on approaches that build and maintain consultation with the Bible as the essence of Christian counselling.

### *Building A Case for the Bible*

It is almost by definition that we must recognize the vital, central role of the Bible in therapy for older people. Clinton and Ohlschlager argue that knowledge is crucial in counseling because it facilitates imparting information and assessment. The authors show wisdom as the know-how to apply the gained knowledge. According to Span, "Scripture can be used in thought stopping, thought shaping, and cognitive disruption" (i). Therefore, wisdom is identifying problems and finding solutions from God's perspective. This involves keen discernment, deep understanding, and sound judgment. Thus, pastors counseling older adults with traumatic experiences should practice seeking knowledge and wisdom from God, thinking like God, and finding God's thoughts in the Bible. This shows that the more the counselor depends on the Word of God, the more they will find God's wisdom and apply it. Proverbs 4:5 says, "Get wisdom and insight! Do not forget or ignore what I say" (RVS).

The Bible, in 2 Timothy 3:16-17, describes itself as "useful for teaching the truth, rebuking error, correcting faults, and giving instruction for a right living so that the person who serves God may be fully qualified and equipped to do every kind of good deed" (RVS). Thus, the wise Christian counselor will use the Bible because it sheds light on right living. Bible is not a spiritual source to be sought or a literary source for quotes. It provides wisdom to live as God pleases. It provides knowledge and wisdom for day-to-day life, as well as how to address our daily life experiences. Psalm 119:105 says, "Your word is a lamp to guide me and a light for my path" (RVS). The Bible is a supernatural power that can be leveraged by pastors to help elderly people to deal with traumatic crises. Hebrews 4:12 says, "the Word of God is alive and active," and when counselors solely rely on it, they will find useful words to help older adults facing traumatic crises.

*Prayer for Awareness of Biblical Teachings*

*Dear God, I know the Bible is your Word and, truly, the only way that those who are older and afflicted with physical and emotional issues, can find a path to recovery and meaning. Please help me and those I counsel to see this and to always consult the scriptures in the search for meaning in life.*

### Pastoral Talk

It follows from the last section, that someone who wants to serve as a Christian counselor must build the knowledge and skills required for what can simply be called "pastoral talk." This means acquiring skills of both interpretation and verbal clarification for one's counselee. Maloney argued, "counselors who use scripture in counseling should be as able at exegeting as they are at expositing . . . [this] assures the counselee that the Bible will be utilized in therapy with as much expertise as will psychodynamics and personality theory" (121).

During the initial pastoral conversations, the Book of Job is useful for its components that could aid the counselee in connecting with their wounded self and discovering fresh outlets for pain. This path may aid in their quest to understand their relationship to God, other people, themselves, and the event they were still dealing with. Approaching the trauma using Job's language in the lingo of the experience of death may prove beneficial.[17]

The trauma of suffering is discussed in the Book of Job. The terrible events in Job's life— the loss of his money and possessions, the unexpected deaths of his children, and the outright

---

[17] For discussion of the relevance of the Book of Job to trauma, see Mathewson.

assault on his health—make it difficult to determine if he was traumatized or suffered from PTSD. His safe haven has been destroyed, making it no longer serve as a safe haven. However, traumas can also be brought on by reactions to the surroundings.

Pastoral conversations involve the exchange of purposeful words targeted at achieving an objective, especially a change in the personal relationship with God. Thus, why is a personal relationship with God important when going through suffering? Pastoral conversations empathize with caring for the people of God and walking beside them regardless of what they are going through. This enables the pastors to understand the needs of the children of God and be able to communicate the word of God in contextually appropriate ways to address their issues.[18] Bible verses should guide pastoral conversations at all times.

*Prayer for Learning Pastoral Talk*

*Dear Lord. Teach me thy ways of interpreting and retelling your teachings from the Scriptures so that the people that I counsel can see Your way and how tp bring their lives into alignment with the Word of God.*

### Developing Good Listening Skills: Pastoral Listening

Just as one must learn pastoral talk, one must also learn pastoral listening! An effective counselor is one who has mastered the art of being a good listener. These skills are developed through training and practicing, which enable counselors to develop a third ear. Older adults experiencing needs a good listener who can keenly listen to them when recounting their traumatic experiences. Good listening is good enough because it allows the counselee to leave the counseling session with effusive thanks because most of the counselor's time has been spent listening rather than reflecting on the spoken words. Pastors may sometimes think that they should have answers

---

[18] For further on communication between pastors and counselees, see Miller, "The spiral staircase."

and advice to offer the counselee after every question or spoken word. However, this is not of considerable significance, considering the target population is older adults with traumatic crises. Thus, listening is significant in this case in order to make the counseling process effective and helpful to older adults.

The Word of God shows us that God listens to us when we pray. And we communicate with God through prayers. The counseling process is anchored on communication skills and so, pastors should learn how to listen carefully to their counselees from the Bible. Psalm 66:19 says, "But God has indeed heard me; he has listened to my prayer" (RVS). To understand the needs of older adults, listening should be considered with utmost care. The verse implies God first listens to us in order to attend to us. To develop strategies to help older adults with traumatic experiences, listening will have to be prioritized to determine the right course of action to take. Thus, if God, in spite of his omniscience, always listens to what people say, the counselor who would follow His example, must also learn to listen actively. In James 1:19, this advice so important to those who would counsel others, resounds: "Wherefor my beloved brethren, let every man be swift to hear, slow to speak" (KJV) and Matthew 11:15 proclaims, "Whoever hath ears, let them hear." These and other verses call on us to listen to others as God listens to us: "The righteous cry, and the Lord hears, and delivereth them out of all their troubles" (Psalm 34:17, KJV)

*Prayer to Be a Good Listener*

*Lord, I am thankful that you always attend to what I say and think and bring me peace thereby. Dear God, provide me the skill and heart to be a good listener too. Teach me to listen well so that I also may guide others to follow in Your path and thereby heal. Amen.*

## 5. Specific Skills for Counselling Practice

This final collection of ideas related to counselling of older people cpould be called the "nitty-gritty" advice. It is about the specific areas of the practice of Christian counselling that the practitioner needs to attend to so that their service is efficient and effective, things we must do on a day-to-day basis.

### *Thankfulness for Being Able to Counsel*

It is important as the counselor proceeds through their heavy and emotional workload to stop and take moments to be grateful for the opportunity to help. It is so easy to get caught up in the hurly-burly of daily schedules and feeling lost amidst so much suffering that we forget just how blessed we and our opportunity to counsel others really is. The Good Samaritan recognized that helping another repays the giver many-fold. So, without hesitation, he paid for the injured man's medical bills out of his own pocket (Luke 10:35). He was effectively saying, "This is my problem, not your concern." By contributing your time, money, and resources to the relief effort, you may help in the same way. By providing small-group support and therapy programs, churches can also be of assistance. A chance to "de-brief" about their losses and painful experiences are necessary for many victims. This form of ownership in life situations involves taking the initiative to bring about desired outcomes. It means not relying on others to care and act to bring positive results out of the counseling process.

Pastors are regarded as the shepherd of the church under the guidance of Jesus Christ the Good Shepherd (John 10:1-18). Pastors should be able to identify the older adults in the church and regularly find out how they are doing with life. This enables the counselors to identify the impacts of traumatic experiences among older adults at the early stages. Early detection of the impacts of traumatic events enables effective management of the consequences, such as anxiety, stress, or depression. This will ensure considerable resources have been used to improve the quality of life among the identified older adults with traumatic experiences.

*Prayer of Thanks for Opportunity to Counsel*

*O God, I worship and honor you, for you are my wonderful creator. You created me with different abilities and placed me on earth for a divine purpose. I bless you for the opportunities you put before me so I can serve you. I hope you will give me a sense of responsibility for myself and the people you will bring into my life. Help me that I will never waste the gifts that you have given to me. Guide me so that I will be productive in my life and the opportunity you have given me as a counselor, in Jesus' name. Amen.*

## Assigning Client Homework

Client homework in counseling refers to the out-of-session activity, which the counselor and counselee agree on because it is designed to help the client to move toward the achievement of the counseling goals. Counseling is time-limited, and clients are empowered to have control over their life situations; thus, the counselees are expected to actively work outside the counseling sessions. In this activity, pastors design assignments that focus on identifying the connections between feelings, thoughts, and actions. Also, clients are asked to record automatic thinking in moments of distress or crisis. Additionally, self-monitoring activities are suggested to extend learning into the client's real world. The counselor's creativity and the client's case of mindful awareness and resources set the limit of the design and nature of homework assignments.

Traumatic experiences cause cognitive problems among older adults; thus, the design of out-of-session activities is intended to help the clients to have better mental health, which significantly affects physical health. Counselors use these structured and focused activities to enable their clients to implement the knowledge their gain in counseling sessions in real-world settings. This helps to make the Christian counseling sessions effective in addressing the issues affecting older adults with traumatic experiences. This shows apart from praying and reading the Bible, pastors need to direct their clients on being actively involved in the counseling process for optimal outcomes.

In the present world, Christian counselors serve in church settings where there is an increase in unbelievers, and believers are constantly inundated with a bombardment of earthly philosophies. Some are deceitfully subtle, and others highly sophisticated. However, the counselors must teach sound doctrine, faithfully refute error, and provide reasonable hope in Christ in the presence of different challenges. Considerably, counselors are regularly engaged in apologetic tasks. Rickett argues: "Besides difficulties exacerbated by the insidious encroachment of the age, a preponderance of problems traditionally addressed by counselors are often a result of bad theology or wrong thinking about God" (1).

Thus, there is a need for Christian counselors to focus on teaching their clients to think rightly about God and help the counselees to replace their unbiblical behaviors and thoughts with living and thinking submitted to Christ's Lordship. Believers who in their old age experience traumatic crises, become exposed to the danger of absorbing the worldly perspectives of the godless within their sphere of influence. Therefore, the counselor must develop skills in responding to and identifying unbiblical systems of thinking and be always prepared to provide an answer that can give hope based on gentleness and reverence. 1 Peter 3:15 says, "Always be prepared to give an answer to everyone who asks you to give the reason for the hope that you have. But do this with gentleness and respect" (NIV).

### *Achieving Selflessness*

Selflessness involves loving other people with an equal measure you would love yourself. It is a practice that counselors should embrace and keep throughout their lives, not only in counseling sessions. This personality will be more useful if pastors make it part of their daily lives. It is not logical to shield someone from the consequences of sinful behaviors as a way of expressing selflessness. Still, the individual will have to repent and change their behavior in order to glorify God. However, with the struggles that older adults experience because of undergoing traumatic events, pastors can selflessly help them to cope with their situations and overcome the related challenges. By doing this, the counselor would have accomplished what is written in the Philemon about considering others more than we consider ourselves. This practice involves going the extra mile to ensure the counselees' needs are met and prioritizing their well-being at all times. It involves being patient and kind and not being envious or rude to other people. In one of his teachings, Jesus used the Good Samaritan parable. The Samaritan had to halt his travels to assist the bleeding guy on the side of the road. He had to put his personal plans on hold to be selfless. We cannot emulate him without being prepared to make the same kind of sacrifice. Don't simply help when it's convenient; help out when it's needed. Philemon 2: 3–5 says, "Do nothing from selfishness or empty conceit, but with humility of mind regard one another as more important than yourselves; do not merely look out for your own personal interests, but also for the interests of others. Have this attitude in yourselves which was also in Christ Jesus"(NASB).

The Samaritan had to attend to his client first before continuing with his journey. He had to find money to pay for the bills at the inn after returning from his journey, not because he was rich but because of selflessness. The more that a counselor recognizes that practicing everyday small details of their work is itself an act or enabling of the act of selflessness.

*Prayer for Selflessness*

*My Lord, help me to choose your way of selflessness and not think only of myself and my own selfish interests as I live my life. Show me how to be more compassionate and put others' interests ahead of my own. Amen.*

### Praying with the Counselee

Prayers are very significant in the Christian life. As I mentioned earlier, we communicate with God through prayers. God requires us to communicate with Him because he is always waiting to listen to us. Daily prayers are essential to individuals, families, and those we pray for.

Prayer plays a significant role in bringing peace into our lives, helping us to know more about God's plans for us, and preventing calamities from coming our way. Therefore, pastors will have to practice planning sessions or days for prayers with their counselees.

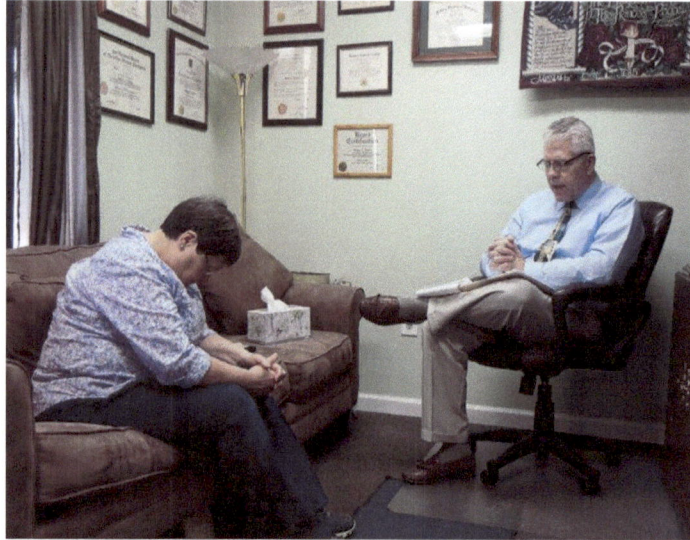

Fig.14. Prayer during Counseling Session with Dr. Rickey Nation, Director of Abundant Life Christian Counseling Services. https://abundantlife4me.org/wp-content/uploads/2015/04/14ˉ12ˉ11ˉ13ˉ27ˉ49_ALCCS_cropped.jpg

Although the counseling period may be limited, time for prayers must be created. This involves a few days of fasting and praying and going to isolated places to pray. We emulate this practice from our Lord Jesus Christ, who regularly went to fast and pray and went to isolated places to pray.

Matthew 17:21 says, "However, this kind does not go out except by prayer and fasting" (NKJV). Some life issues can be overcome by prayer and fasting. We do not have any other option than taking time to pray. Jesus was God in human form while on earth, and he could cry loudly and pray with tears to God the Father because he was the only one who could save Him (Hebrews 5:11). If Jesus could live and pray in this manner, as human beings we desperately need God's help in each moment of our lives.

***Prayer About Praying***

*Dear Heavenly Father, you are all-powerful and all-knowing. You know the intensity of life issues we go through, and you are powerful in delivering me from any distress, anxiety, and whatever situation. God, I thank you because you are able to fight all our battles. You say in Matthew 11:28, "Come to me, all of you who are tired from carrying heavy loads, and I will give you rest." I come to you, God, to find rest because I am crushed and tired in the name of Jesus. Amen.*

## *Viewing Our Lives with God's Perspective*

We honor Bible by using it according to God's intent, and we honor human life when we acknowledge it as God intends. God created us in a way that we dynamically react to life situations, and our reaction is multifaceted. The nature of people is to think, want and choose. People need their minds directed and their hearts captured. God gave people free will; thus, people desire to make new choices and be shown what results they will have from their choices. Pastors should understand that older adults need help in understanding the impacts of their private thoughts in relation to important people in their lives, as well as how events in their past lives affect their present lives.

Pastors should be carried by love and caring heart to help older adults understand themselves and find solutions to their present situations. Pastors should handle older adults with traumatic experiences with enough care and pray to God to help them to have the right knowledge and wisdom to deal with them.

***Prayer on Seeing Human Life as God Does***

*Mighty God, I honor you for creating us with a divine purpose. You value us more than any other creation because we praise and worship you. You say in Isaiah 49:16 that you have engraved us on your palms and let your goodness and mercy follow us throughout our lives. I thank you for how you value me to the point of letting your only begotten Son die for my sins. Help me to love you and care about the people around me. In the name of Jesus Christ, I pray, Amen.*

## Developing Problem-Solving Skills

Counseling involves people who come to seek help because they are struggling with a certain problem. When Christians are not doing well in their lives, they find pastors for help. Thus, counseling is designed in response to an identified problem in a person's life. An effective counselor will successfully address problems when they are always prepared. Shaw et al. (2005) state: "Christian will maintain an attitude of spiritual readiness with his heart and mind continually open to guidance from the Holy Spirit." Problem-solving skills are developed over time, and pastors need to practice this activity to make counseling sessions successful.

Counselors can learn from Apostle Paul the skills to solve problems. These skills should be derived from Biblical teachings. Christians build their lives on the Word of God. Proverbs 3:5 "Trust in the Lord with all your heart and lean not on your own understanding" (NIV). When these skills are developed based on the Bible, God will be honored because this implies that the Word of God informs everything conducted in the counseling sessions.

### Prayer to Be Guided by Christ in Problem-Solving

*Dear Father, I thank you for your guidance in my life. I honor you and solely rely on you because you are the best for me. The world is full of philosophies that try to lead us astray and fail to glorify you throughout our lives. When the world tries to lure me to its wisdom and knowledge, I pray to empower me and grant me knowledge and wisdom that is hidden in you, Jesus Christ who said in Colossians 2:3. "Help me to do everything in my life according to your revelation and guidance in order to be glorified and honor." In Jesus' name. Amen.*

## Professional Development

Professional development is perceived as gaining knowledge and skills and trying to keep up to up-to-date managerially, clinically, and professionally. Studies[19] show this is the main strategy

---

[19] See Pedhu for research on improving performance among pastoral counselors.

used by counselors to continually improve their performance in counseling practice. Rønnestad et al. offer a description of professional development as "changes in the skillfulness, attitudes, cognitive capacities, emotional and interpersonal functioning and vocational identity of professional counselors" (214). Professional development is considered a significant practice that allows counselors to attain a high standard required to assist the target population in dealing with the implications of their traumatic experiences. Pastoral counselors are required to have specific training, knowledge, and skill to perform the counseling practice effectively.

Proverbs 22:29 says: "Do you see a person skilled in his work? He will stand in the presence of kings. He will not stand in the presence of the unknown" (CSB). This verse shows us that God supports skill development. When one is skillful in their area of practice, it enables them to have an excellent performance. David is an example of a skillful man who stood before kings. He could play his harp skillfully that he was brought before king Saul to help him deal with evil spirits. Daniel was skillful in interpreting dreams that he was brought before King Belshazzar. Joseph was brought before Pharaoh. Thus, requires us to excel in

*Prayer for Developing Professionally*

*Dear Father, I thank you because you give us gifts so that we may serve and glorify you. You enable us to excel in whatever we do for your glory. You always make the head those who obey and worship you. Father, you have given me the grace to be counseling people. I do this as a service to you. I pray that you will make me excel in this practice for your glory, Lord. Where I am weak or underperforming, help me to improve, in Jesus' name. Amen.*

*Performance Evaluation*

For a better understanding of pastoral counseling effectiveness, it is imperative for pastors involved in counseling elderly people with traumatic experiences to evaluate their performance. This implies pastoral counselors must continually evaluate themselves in order to identify their strengths and weaknesses. Pedhu (2020) states, "The more pastoral counselors evaluate their performance through both self-evaluation and professional evaluation by professionals, the higher the chance of their success in helping clients."

The process of performance evaluation involves analyzing the pastor's skills, personal strengths, and limitations. The awareness established through this process will enable pastors to know how they are helpful to older adults undergoing traumatic crises. Counseling practice aims to help the target population, and poor performance contributes to harmful outcomes for the individuals. Thus, this practice is necessary to ensure the best counseling services are provided to the target population. Bible shows us that God is performance-conscious. Colossians 3:23 tells us, "Work hard and cheerfully at all you do, just as though you were working for the Lord and not merely for your masters" (TLB). Thus, quality performance is a requirement in pastoral counseling practice.

*Prayer for Improving Performance*

*Dear heavenly Father, you do not intend for anyone of us to be lazy in what we do. We know that we do not need to support you to make our lives better, but you require us to use the abilities that you have given us. While using gifts and abilities you have given us, you need us to be conscious enough for better performance, and in everything we do, we should do as we are serving our Lord. Father, help me continually improve my skills to serve your people better, and make me a useful vessel in this ministry. In the name of Jesus, I pray. Amen.*

*Supervision*

Traumatic experiences have a great potential to make an individual vulnerable to developing mental health problems. Studies show trauma directly causes posttraumatic stress disorder (PTSD). Due to these health problems, some people end up in drug abuse or self-harm to cope with difficult emotions and memories.[20] Therefore, counseling practice plays an essential role

---

[20] Krause discusses the nature of lifetime trauma in late life and the role of prayer in relieving distress.

in enabling elderly people to manage mental health problems that are contributed by traumatic crises. Hence, supervision is an activity that should be considered to make the counseling services objective and effective. Ward and House argue that supervision is a crucial part of counseling practice and plays a central role in continual professional development and counselor education for pastoral counselors. When supervision is integrated into pastoral counseling, it provides continual support to pastors to develop, monitor, and refine their skills. In the presence of supervision, pastoral counselors can improve their knowledge base and skills, ensure ethical and responsible practice, and monitor their professional competence and self-care. This activity is imperative because it allows the supervisor and supervisee to learn from one another.

We can refer to the basis of supervision in the Christianity community as how Jesus poured out his life into the lives of his disciple. Jesus went about significantly impacting people's lives. Learning from Jesus and supervision brings growth, cooperation, fellowship, and partnership. When these attributes are characterized in counseling practice, the counselees are able to benefit from the process and enjoy a quality life and health (emotionally, mentally, and physically).

*Prayer for Jesus's Guidance and Teaching*

*Dear Lord Jesus, I honor you as my master. I pray that you call me to be your faithful servant. It is a great privilege to serve you, Lord of lords. I humble myself to you so that you will teach me what I must know to serve you diligently. Give me the grace to obey those who you put above me; through your holy name I pray. Amen.*

### Consultation with Other Christian Counselors

I encourage pastors to consult with their colleagues, particularly the experienced and senior counselors in the Christian community. Pastoral counselors are guaranteed to benefit from this practice by gaining new insights concerning counseling cases they are dealing with. Consultation practice regarding a certain counseling case helps pastoral counselors to get useful feedback, which is meaningful for the whole counseling process.[21] Further, studies show consultation contributes to greater commitment and awareness because it increases a better understanding of the decision-making process in counseling practice. Also, consultation improves working relationships among pastoral counselors, leading to increased cooperation and trust.

When dealing with older adults with traumatic experiences, it is imperative to carefully consider the decisions that are made to improve their later lives. Thus, consultation is a significant factor to consider before making decisions in order to make the counseling process effective. Proverbs 15:22 says, "Without consultation, plans are frustrated, but with many counselors, they succeed." (NASB). Knowledge will be beneficial to us when we apply it. God wants us to succeed in what we do, and if the counseling process can be effective through consultation, then why would counselors fail to seek advice? Thus, this activity should be factored into counseling practice to develop a community that fears God and depends on Him alone.

***Prayer to Lead and Help Those in Need***

*Dear Holy Spirit, I thank you for your counsel and direction. I humble myself to you to yield to God's will. I cannot serve better and please God without your help. I pray to lead me to help people when I am seeking advice. Take control of me and my thoughts. In the name of Jesus Christ, I pray. Amen.*

### Reviewing Counselee Well-Being Outcomes

Reviewing in counseling involves monitoring the counselee's progress, or lack of it. The counselor literally reviews how the counselee is faring with the counseling process. Counseling practice is goal-oriented, and counselors must ensure they are on the right track to achieve the set goals. Reviewing the progress of the clients helps to determine the effectiveness of the counseling

---

[21] On consultation practice and the role of professional development in strengthening it, see Rønnestad et al.

services. When dealing with older adults with traumatic experiences, the goals would be; changed lifestyles, change the impact of the immediate traumatic crisis, increase confidence to make personal decisions, improve relationships, and improve knowledge on managing stress and anxiety. When a review is done, it allows the counselor to determine the effectiveness and appropriateness of the current systems and services. This allows pastoral counselors to decide whether to change or maintain the current services and systems.

The Bible teaches about progressing to complete transformation. Philippians 1:6 says, "I am sure of this, that He who started a good work in you will carry it on to completion until the day of Christ Jesus" (HCSB). And, when you read Psalm 138:8, the Psalmist tells us that God perfects what concerns Him. Therefore, we can conclude that God delights in his children's positive progression. Similarly, a successful counseling practice should involve the regular review, especially of the client's progress.

The well-being of older adults is associated with several family-, social-, and health-related benefits.[22] For instance, increased levels of well-being are associated with decreased risk of illness, injury, and disease; speedier recovery; better immune functioning; and increased longevity. The aim of the counseling practice involving older adults is to achieve considerably higher levels of well-being. Older adults represent a socially accurate and relevant depiction of the quality of pastoral counseling and care provided to them in a Christian community. Thus, this review is essential for community development and improvement.

The review concerning the well-being outcomes of older adults with traumatic crises would be assessed by using several components, including the promotion of well-being and health;

---

[22] This classification has been developed by the Centers for Disease Control and Prevention (CDC) in "Social support and health-related quality of life among older adults--Missouri, 2000."

emotional, spiritual, and physical care; resilience; and social capital within the Christian community (Mullen et al.). This review will contribute not only to the well-being of the target population but also to the general Christian community as a whole. Counseling practice is a form of expressing love for one another and a way of serving the living God. Thus, from this practice, God can act according to His word in Exodus 23:25, which says; "So you shall serve the LORD your God, and He will bless your bread and your water. And I will take away sickness from among you" (MSB).

*Prayer for Progress in Counseling Effectiveness*

*Dear God, I thank you for teaching us from the moment of planting a seed to harvesting grains. When a seed is sowed, it must grow into a plant that brings forth fruits of grain. Father, I pray to enable our counseling sessions to be fruitful. Give us cooperation and patience to achieve this practice's desired outcomes, in Jesus' name. Amen.*

### Using Available Data to Develop Best Counseling Practices

Research is important in counseling practice because it improves the appropriateness and effectiveness of the process. Pastoral counselors can leverage quantitative and qualitative data analysis and interpretation to gain information useful to develop best counseling practices and optimize counseling outcomes. Wester et al. state: "Research provides evidence for the range of issues where therapy can be effective and the positive outcomes for clients." (280). Considering research findings in the counseling process is imperative because it helps develop evidence-based practices to help older adults with traumatic crises. Also, quantitative and qualitative data can be used by pastoral counselors to develop counseling frameworks or programs that are comprehensive, and data driven. Thus, it will be guaranteed that any decision made during the counseling process will bring out positive outcomes for the target population.

Using data in Christian counseling will help older adults with traumatic experiences to have a successful healing process. This implies the strategies that pastoral counselors will use to help these people will be biblically and scientifically proven. God has given us the ability to learn and acquire knowledge that we can utilize to make our lives better. Thus, the knowledge that can be gained from research integrated with Biblical knowledge will contribute to better and desired outcomes among the target population. Bible is not a collection of research methodology; however, it lays a basis for conducting research from a Biblical perspective. Bible verses support this activity: Acts 17:11; 1 Thessalonians 5:21; John 5:39; and Deuteronomy 13:14.

### *Enabling Counselees to Reflect on their Pastoral Counseling Practices*

Older adults with traumatic crises must clarify their understanding of their pastoral counseling role and how their relationships and own actions can improve or harm their well-being. The counseling process involving older adults with traumatic experiences is influenced by personal qualities and their relationships; the counselee's participation and its ability to promote meaningful cooperation and positive counseling experiences; the church's organizational structure and its ability to offer support, safety, guidance, trust, and challenge; and connections with the broader Christian community. This activity aims to actively involve the counselee in the counseling process by empowering them to take action about their situation. This activity enables the counselee to feel they are still in control of their lives rather than being controlled to behave in a certain way.

God created us with different abilities and predestined different lives for each of us. When pastoral counselor tries to enable older adults it pleases God, because it implies an appreciation of how God made us diversely. Paul and Timothy provide us with a real-life case study of how a counselor can enable their clients to become better in their lives. Paul encouraged Timothy to focus on nourishment from God's word, a mission-minded approach, and training in godliness. These are practices that required Timothy to keep throughout his life. Paul empowered Timothy with words and acted as a mentor until Timothy became a bishop. 2 Timothy 1:13 says, "Hold to the standard of sound teaching that you have heard from me" (NRSV). Similarly, a pastoral counselor has to enable older adults with traumatic crises to put into practice the lessons they learn from counseling sessions and reflect on how they are doing between the sessions. This enables them to be self-driven and intrinsically motivated to improve their later lives.

*Prayer for Reflection*

*Dear Lord, I thank you for you have created an opportunity to better my life and develop the ability to overcome the challenges I am facing in my life. Thank you for the people you have brought into my life to help me handle my current situation. Above all, I know you are beside me. Please help me to come out of this victoriously and be glorified for the useful persons you have a place in my life. In Jesus' name, Amen.*

*Developing Decision-Making Skills*

Pastoral counselors should be able to devise a decision-making model in counseling sessions, especially when dealing with delicate target populations such as older adults with traumatic crises. The decision-making skills that pastoral counselors should enable them to envision counseling as a three-stage process: the problem definition phase, the work phase, and the action phase. The problem definition phase involves considering alternative definitions of the problem presented by the client and encouraging them to commit to one of the definitions. The work phase involves the pastoral counselor helping the counselee to look at the problem from various perspectives and finding the appropriate solutions. During the action phase, the client makes a decision on what solution to test within their specified environment.

The decision-making process in pastoral counseling is significant for getting desired outcomes. Pastoral counselors should be in a position to understand the context of the presented problem, make plans, identify the "who" and "why," weigh the pros and cons, consider alternatives, limit available choices, set deadlines, evaluate outcomes, and learn from the experience. When these skills are epitomized in the counseling process, without doubt, the client will have far much benefited from the process. These skills can be learned and practiced. Each pastoral counselor should endeavor to have these skills.

Most importantly, counselors should consider Biblical principles of decision-making. For instance, Proverbs 2:6 says, "For the LORD gives wisdom; from his mouth come knowledge and understanding" (NIV). When deciding, pastoral counselors should seek God's wisdom. Also, the counselors should make their decisions in line with Philippians 4:8, which says, "Finally, brothers and sisters, whatever is true, whatever is noble, whatever is right, whatever is pure, whatever is lovely, whatever is admirable—if anything is excellent or praiseworthy—think about such things" (NIV).

### *Arranging Conferences or Meetings*

Previously, I addressed the need for engaging community in counseling practice to contribute to providing social support to older adults with traumatic crises. Moreover, it is imperative to organize meetings specifically with older adults with traumatic experiences. This will be enabled by identifying these people and strategizing how to reach out to the identified individuals. The pastoral counselor will devise a mechanism to send them invitations with enough information about why they are invited to such meetings. When people experiencing similar problems are brought together, it helps in reducing the intensity of the implications of those problems. These interactions enable the target population to develop the courage and confidence to face their issues. Also, this interaction develops unity to forge forward in a spirit of overcoming challenges associated with trauma. Thus, pastoral counselors should consider making such arrangements to make the counseling process appropriate and effective for the target population.

Paul tells the believers of Philippi, "Whatever happens, conduct yourselves in a manner worthy of the gospel of Christ. Then, whether I come and see you or only hear about you in my absence, I will know that you stand firm in the one Spirit, [a] striving together as one for the faith of the gospel" (Philippians 1:27, NIV). Thus, although the challenges the people face, they need to come together as a sign of unity to strengthen one another in faith. As we are referred to as the body of Christ, and Jesus is the Head, we need always to stay close to one another despite the challenges of life we face. And, in staying together, counseling practice will be feasible.

## CONCLUSION

Christian counseling is an effective way to help older adults experiencing a traumatic crisis. By utilizing biblical techniques, such as Proverbs 12:25, Psalm 103:17-18, Romans 8:28, and Isaiah 43:2, counselors can help older adults to find strength and solace in God. Counselors should also focus on helping older adults to build a relationship with God and to take practical steps to move forward. Through Christian counseling, older adults can gain the strength and courage they need to move forward. Christian counseling for older adults is a form of therapy that seeks to help older adults process and heal from traumatic experiences. It combines traditional counseling techniques with Scripture and biblical teachings to provide comfort and healing. This type of counseling is especially beneficial for older adults who are struggling with traumatic crises, such as grief, anxiety, loneliness, and spiritual confusion. using case studies and biblical techniques, Christian counseling can help older adults find healing and hope in the grace and love of God.

## WORKS CITED AND CONSULTED

Adler, Alfred. *The Individual Psychology of Allred Adler*, edited by Heinz L. Ansbacher and Rowena R. Ansbacher. Basic Books, 1956.

American Association of Christian Counselors. *AACC Counselor Toolbox.* 2021 https://www.aacc.net/resources/toolbox/

Anandarajah, G. "Doing a Culturally Sensitive Spiritual Assessment: Recognizing Spiritual Themes and Using the HOPE Questions." *AMA Journal of Ethics—Virtual Mentor*, vol. 7, no. 5, 2005, pp. 371–374. https://doi.org/10.1001/virtualmentor.2005.7.5.cprl1-0505.

Brady, Alec, and David Raines. "Dynamic hierarchies: a control system paradigm for exposure therapy." *The Cognitive Behaviour Therapist*, vol. 2, no. 1, 2009, pp 51–62.

Buechner, Frederick K. *Wishful Thinking: A Theological ABC.* HarperCollins. 1978.

Centers for Disease Control and Prevention (CDC). "Social support and health-related quality of life among older adults--Missouri, 2000." *MMWR Morbidity & Mortality Weekly Report*, vol. 54, no. 17, May 2005, pp. 433-437.

Chand, Suma P., Daniel P. Kuckel, and Martin R. Huecker. "Cognitive behavior therapy." *StatPearls [Internet]*. StatPearls Publishing, 2022.

Christian Counseling & Educational Foundation. *Information page.* 2009. Retrieved from https://www.ccef.org/

Clinton, Tim, and Ron Hawkins. *The Popular Encyclopedia of Christian Counseling: An Indispensable Tool for Helping People with Their Problems.* Harvest House Publishers, 2011.

Clinton, Timothy, and George Ohlschlager, eds. *Competent Christian Counseling, Volume One: Foundations and Practice of Compassionate Soul Care.* Waterbrook, 2002.

Danielson, Ramona A., and Susan Ray-Degges. "Aging in place among older adults with histories of traumatic experiences: A scoping review." *The Gerontologist* 62, no. 1 (2022): e1‑e16.

Dein, Simon. "The Faith of Patients." Presentation given at the Annual Meeting of the Royal College of Psychiatrists, Liverpool, UK , June 2009 https://www.rcpsych.ac.uk/docs/default-source/members/sigs/spirituality-spsig/spirituality-special-interest-group-publications-dein-the-faith-of-patients.pdf?sfvrsn=22389636_2

de Rijk, Angelique et al. "The challenge of return to work in workers with cancer: Employer priorities despite variation in social policies related to work and     health." *Journal     of Cancer Survivorship*, vol. 14, no. 2, 2020, pp. 188–199. https://doi.org/10.1007/s11764-019-00829-y

Dedeli, Ozden, and Gulten Kaptan. "Spirituality and Religion in Pain and Pain Management." *Health Psychology Research*, vol. 1, no. 3, 23 Sept. 2013, p. 154–159. https://doi.org/10.4081/hpr.2013.1448

Delgado, Cheryl. "A discussion of the concept of spirituality." *Nursing Science Quarterly*, vol. 18, no. 2, Apr. 2005, 157–162. https://doi.org/10.1177/0894318405274828

Don'L, Blevins. "A Faith-Based Intervention to Address Social Isolation and Loneliness in Older Adults." *Journal of Christian Nursing*, vol. 40, no. 1, Jan./Mar 2023) pp. 28–35. https://doi.org/10.1097/CNJ.0000000000001023

Dunn, Dana S. "A Psych-Wise Guide to Navigating Social Life." *PsycCRITIQUES*, vol. 61, no. 12, 2016, https://doi.org/10.1037/a0040215

Friedman, Edwin H. *A Failure of Nerve: Leadership in the Age of the Quick Fix*. Church Publishing, 2007.

Garabedian, M. (2017). "Paul Tillich: The courage to be." *Encyclopedia of Christian Education* edited by Oord (Ed.), (pp. 1-2). Rowman & Littlefield Publishers

Geretic, K. E., & Kennedy, G. (Eds.). *Mental health care for older adults* (3rd ed.). New York: Norton, 2012.

Got Questions. "What is Psychoanalytic Theory, and is it Biblical?" https://www.gotquestions.org/psychoanalytic-theory.html

Harris, Gordon. *The Central Event View of Human History Model (CEM): An Apologetic for a Christ-Centered Christian View of Human History.* 2017. Liberty University. PhD Dissertation.

Heart Talk Biblical Counseling. "The Biblical Counseling Process," n.d. Retrieved December 18, 2022, from https://www.hearttalkcounseling.com/the-biblical-counseling-process/

Hughes, Justin K. "A Biblical Rationale for Exposure Therapy" [Blog]. https://www.justinkhughes.com/jog/a-biblical-rationale-for-exposure-therapy/

Jones, Stanton L. and Richard E. Buttman. *Modern Psychotherapies: A Comprehensive Christian Appraisal.* 2nd ed., IVP Academic, 2011.

Kellemen, Bob. *Biblical Counseling and the Church: God's Care Through God's People.* Zondervan, 2015.

Kennedy, Gary. "Mental Health Care for Older Adults." In *Mental Health and Aging: An Evidence-Based Approach.* Edited by S. J. Schulz, & J. C. Breckenridge, Routledge, 2018, pp. 155–184.

Kohls, Benjamin. "Emotional Wellness: Holistic Care for God's Workmanship." Essay for Wisconsin Lutheran Seminary. 2021. http://essays.wisluthsem.org:8080/handle/123456789/6671

Koenig, Harold,.G. "Aging and spirituality and religion." In *Mental health care for older adults* (3rd ed., pp. 77-103). New York: Norton.

Kövecses, Zoltán. *Emotion Concepts*. Springer Science & Business Media, 2012.

Krause, Neal. "Lifetime Trauma, Prayer, and Psychological Distress in Late Life." *International Journal for the Psychology of Religion*. vol.19, no.1, 2009, pp.55–72. https://doi.org/10.1080/10508610802471112

Lamothe, Ryan W. "God representations as transitional subjects." *Psychoanalytic Review*, vol. 97, no. 3, 2010, pp. 425–449. https://doi.org/10.1521/prev.2010.97.3.425.

Levers, Lisa Lopez. *Trauma Counseling: Theories and Interventions*. Springer Publishing Company, 2012.

Lindridge, Andrew. *Keeping the Faith: Spirituality and Recovery from Mental Health Problems*. Mental Health Foundation, London, UK., 2007.

MacDonald, James W., et al. eds. *Christ-Centered Biblical Counseling: Changing Lives With God's Changeless Truth*. Harvest House Publishers, 2013.

Maloney, H. Newton. The clinical assessment of optimal religious functioning. *Review of Religious Research*, vol. 30, no. 1, 1985, pp. 3–17.

Martin, Jeremiah T. et al. "'Normal' vital signs belie occult hypoperfusion in geriatric trauma patients." *The American Surgeon*, vol. 76, no. 1, 2010, pp. 65–69. https://doi.org/10.1177/000313481007600113

Maschi, Tina et al. "Trauma, stress, grief, loss, and separation among older adults in prison: The protective role of coping resources on physical and mental well-being." *Journal of Crime and Justice*, vol. 38, no. 1, 2015, pp. 113–136.

Mathewson, Dan. "Between testimony and interpretation: The Book of Job in post-Holocaust, Jewish theological reflection." *Studies in the Literary Imagination* 41, no. 2 (2008):

17. Mazokopakis, Elias E. "Music as a Medicine for the Soul in Bible and Christian Patristic Tradition." *Journal of Religion & Health*, vol. 59, no. 3, 2020, pp. 1217–1219. https://doi.org/10.1007/s10943-018-0738-4

McDonald, Dean. "The Emotional Intelligence of Jesus: Relational Smarts for Religious Leaders, by." *Reflective Practice: Formation and Supervision in Ministry*, vol 36,

McGwin, Gerald Jr. et al., "Preexisting conditions and mortality in older trauma patients" *Journal of Trauma: Injury, Infection, and Critical Care*, vol. 56, no. 6, 2004, pp. 1291–1296. https://doi.org/10.1097/01.TA.0000089354.02065.D0

Menkel-Meadow, Carrie. "Critical Moments Reconsidered: When We Say Yes and When We Say No." *Negotiation Journal*, vol. 36, no. 2, 23 Mar. 2020, pp. 233–241, https://doi.org/10.1111/nejo.12311.

Mid-America Institute for Nouthetic Studies. "Dr. Jay E. Adams." 2019. http://www.nouthetic.org/about-ins/our-faculty/8-about-ins/6-jay-adams-biography\

Miller, Andrew J. "The spiral staircase: a narrative approach to pastoral conversation." *Journal of Pastoral Care & Counseling* 70, no. 1 (2016): 26-33.

Mullen, Patrick R. et al. "Emotional intelligence and leadership attributes of school counselor trainees." *Counselor Education and Supervision*, vol. 58, no. 2, 2019, pp. 112–126. https://doi.org/10.1002/ceas.12135

National Institute on Aging. *Aging and Trauma*. 2021.https://www.nia.nih.gov/health/aging-and-trauma .

Norcross, John C. *Psychotherapy Relationships That Work: Therapist Contributions and Responsiveness to Patients*. Oxford University Press, 2002.

O'Leary, Eleanor. *Counseling older adults*. Routledge, 2020.

Oswald, Frank, and Graham D. Rowles. "Beyond the relocation trauma in old age: New trends in elders' residential decisions." In *New Dynamics in Old Age Individual, Environmental, and Societal Perspectives*, pp. 127–152. Routledge, 2017.

Oswald, Roy M., and Arland Jacobson. *The Emotional Intelligence of Jesus: Relational Smarts for Religious Leaders*. Rowman & Littlefield, 2015.

Pearce, Michelle J., et al. "Religiously Integrated Cognitive Behavioral Therapy: A New Method of Treatment for Major Depression in Patients with Chronic Medical Illness." *Psychotherapy,* vol. 52, no.1, 2015, pp. 56–66. https://doi.org/10.1037/a0036448

Pedhu, Yoseph. "Improving performance: What pastoral counselors can do." *COUNS-EDU: The International Journal of Counseling and Education* 5, no. 1 (2020): 29-38.

Pittman, Chanté L. (2022). *The Integration of Christian Values into Cognitive Behavioral Therapy*. 2022, The Chicago School of Professional Psychology, PhD Dissertation. *Proques*t, https://www.proquest.com/openview/d391bb06d09522f42b54d9520e294808/1?pq-origsite=gscholar&cbl=18750&diss=y

Rickett, R. Brian. "Biblical Counseling & Apologetics BC 509: Course Introduction." The Master's College, Santa Clarita, CA. https://www.academia.edu/12616747/BC_509_BIBLICAL_COUNSELING_and_APOL OGETICS

Rønnestad, Michael H. et al. "The Professional Development of Counsellors and Psychotherapists: Implications of Empirical Studies for Supervision, Training and Practice." *Counseling & Psychotherapy Research*, vol. 19, no. 3, 2019, pp. 214–230. https://doi.org/10.1002/capr.12198

Ryan, E. B. et al. "Psycholinguistic and Social Psychological Components of Communication by and With the Elderly." *Language and Communication*, vol. 6, no. 1, pp. 1–24.

Sabra, Kimberly. *Understanding the Experiences of Spirituality in Post-Traumatic Growth for Older Adults: A Narrative Approach.* 2020. Michigan School of Psychology, PhD dissertation.

Savage, David G. "Court Ruling That Freed Clergy from Liability for Advice Allowed to Stand." *Los Angeles Times*, April 4, 1989. https://www.latimes.com/archives/la-xpm-1989-04-04-mn-952-story.html

Shafranke, Edward P. "Spiritually Oriented Psychodynamic Psychotherapy." *Journal of Clinical Psychology,* vol. 65, no. 2, 2009, pp. 147–157. https://doi.org/10.1002/jclp.20565.

Shaw, Annick et al. "Religion, Spirituality, and Posttraumatic Growth: A Systematic Review." *Mental Health, Religion & Culture*, vol. 8, no. 1, 2005, pp. 1–11. https://doi.org/10.1080/1367467032000157981

Span, A. Tim. *Using Scripture in Counselling Evangelicals.* 2009. Waterloo Lutheran Seminary. Thesis, Master of Theology in Pastoral Counseling. https://scholars.wlu.ca/cgi/viewcontent.cgi?article=1949&context=etd

Terrion, Jenepher L., and Martine Lagacé. "Communication as Precursor and Consequence of Subjective Social Capital in Older People: A New Perspective on the Communication Predicament Model." *Social Theory & Health*, vol. 6, 2008), pp. 239–249. https://doi.org/10.1057/sth.2008.8

Turgut, Tuğba, and E. K. Ş. İ. Füsun. "Spiritually-oriented cognitive-behavioral family therapy." *Spiritual Psychology and Counseling*, vol. 5, no.1, 2020, pp. 87–111.

Van Belle, Harry A. "Philosophical Roots of Person-Centered Therapy in the History of Western Thought." *The Person-Centered Journal*, vol. 12, no 1–2, 2005, pp. 50–60. https://www.adpca.org/wp-content/uploads/2020/11/12_1_7.pdf

Walker, Donald F., et al. "Therapists' Use of Religious and Spiritual Interventions in Christian Counseling: A Preliminary Report." *Counseling & Values*, vol. 49, no. 2, 2005, pp.107–119. https://doi.org/10.1002/j.2161-007X.2005.tb00257.x

Weidmann, Josh. "7 Essential Elements of a First Session in Biblical Counseling." https://joshweidmann.com/essential-elements-of-a-first-session-in-biblical-counseling/

Wester, Kelly L., et al. "Research Quality: Critique of Quantitative Articles in the Journal of Counseling & Development." *Journal of Counseling & Development*, vol. 91, no. 3, 2013, pp. 280–290. https://doi.org/10.1002/j.1556-6676.2013.00096.x

Worthington, Everett L., Jr. *Marriage Counseling: A Christian Approach to Counseling Couples*. InterVarsity Press, 2019

Zust, Barbara L., et al. "Evangelical Christian Pastors' Lived Experience of Counseling Victims/Survivors of Domestic Violence. *Pastoral Psychology*, vol. 66, no. 5, 2017, pp. 675–687. https://doi.org/10.1007/s11089-017-0781-1.

www.ingramcontent.com/pod-product-compliance
Lightning Source LLC
Chambersburg PA
CBHW060813270326
41929CB00002B/18